zuckerbook

Jerry Zucker Middle School of Science

The Zuckerbook Project

2014/15

faculty advisor
Mr. Erik J. Hilden

internal production
Christina Smith editor
Matthew Greene art director
Janiah Black copywriter
Jessica Estevez copywriter
Daniel Hernandez Perianez copywriter

external production
Patrick Myers production lead
Terry Dela Cruz team member
Zenaida Ingram team member
Xavier Henlon team member

fundraising
Fanny Villasenor team leader
Jalynn Henryhand co-leader
Tynerria Johnson fundraiser
Keirra Ancrum fundraiser
Tyrell Alston fundraiser
David Cattles fundraiser

public relations
Kayla Cannady public relations lead
Samiyah Frasier team member
Keyonne' McKnight team member

cover art Ben Holmes

Copyright 2015 by **The Zuckerbook Project** in concert with:

The Students of Jerry Zucker Middle School of Science
6401 Dorchester Road, North Charleston, South Carolina 29418
Principal: Jacob Perlmutter

ISBN: 978-0-692-59743-9

Printed in the United States of America

Dedication

This work is dedicated to the students
who created each piece that is
contained within these pages.
Their words, their artwork, their spirits
and their energies bring this work to life.
May their voices always be heard.

Community Involvement

Endeavors such as these are evidence of the great things that can
happen when a community pulls together in the face of adversity and
produces a testament to the voices of their children. Without the support
of our community, this would not have been possible, and without further
support, future endeavors may not come to pass. We have had a lot of
support this year, but we can always use more, as is true of any non-
profit activity. If you are interested in donating to The Zuckerbook Project
or are interested in volunteering to help in any way, please feel free to get
in touch. I can be reached at erik_hilden@charleston.k12.sc.us or at the
following address:

The Zuckerbook Project c/o
Jerry Zucker Middle School of Science
6401 Dorchester Rd. Room 159
North Charleston, SC 29418
843-767-8383 ext. 25614

Acknowledgements

"Thank You" pages can sound cheesy. Perhaps there is no way around that. I don't know. But, they are a necessary part of the process, as without the fine folks listed here, there would probably not be a Zuckerbook this year.

Mr. Perlmutter, our esteemed principal and leader, threw his support behind us and gave us a lot of leeway in fund raising and how we chose to organize The Zuckerbook Project, letting it be an independent not-for-profit business run by the students and monitored (closely) by myself. **Mr. White** and **Mr. Maybank** gave me a daily break after the class was up and running. **Mr. Crankfield** and **Ms. Knox** helped us with our table when we sold "cookie grams" to raise funds. **Ms. Mustipher, Ms. Macomber, Ms. Guider, Ms. Gregory**, **Ms. Carasik**, and **Mr. Aiello** funneled creative work our way. **The entire faculty of Zucker Middle School** tolerated our pleas for donations and our fund raising activities, and **the janitorial staff** cleaned up after us with their usual dedication and aplomb.

Dr. Clark G. Hilden, my father and the inspiration behind the Cultural Anthropology class that became The Zuckerbook Project, deserves special notice for not only his moral support, but also for his financial support, as does my dear friend **Brent Mills**, who was touched by what we were doing and wanted to make sure it came to fruition. Both of these men brought us to our fund raising goal and beyond with their generous donations and their appreciation for the underlying purpose of The Zuckerbook Project, which is best stated by our mission statement:

The Mission of The Zuckerbook Project is to produce the very highest quality Student Publication of Literary Works intermingled with Visual Art, Research, Editorials of Student Interest, and Expository Works while Remaining Faithful to the Zucker Middle School Student Experience, and then distribute it to the community, so that our voices may be heard. Open it and read…

Ms. Sarah Douglas, a dear friend, colleague, and reading/writing enthusiast, deserves special mention for being involved with the first two issues, "Dude, It's A Magazine," and the first "Zuckerbook." She gathered the lion's share of student work and collected the artwork and, the moment I stated at that first faculty meeting in August of 2011 that I wanted to run a Literary Magazine Club, jumped right over and declared without hesitation that I had stolen her idea and we had best work together to make this happen. She has been a driving force from the beginning, and though her hands have not touched this issue, her spirit is more than included, and always will be.

Mr. James Brooks, guidance counselor, helped me staff my class with gifted students whom he thought would be perfect for a project such as Zuckerbook, and I will always be grateful for his support and contribution to our staff. Without him, we would not have had a Zuckerbook this year.

But, the biggest thank you of all has to go to the **students**, who dug deep into their own pockets and donated dollar after dollar to fund this year's offering. Without their support and their remarkable work, none of this would have been possible. Thank you, one and all, for making our dreams come true.

-- *Mr. Erik J. Hilden, April 2nd, 2015*

zuckerbook

Contents

1 Haiku

Janet Vasquez

Between the two trees,
Looking up at the branches
Which one should we climb?

Jennifer Aleman

Falling to the ground
I watch the leaf settle down
In a bed of brown

Jackie Fulton

Today is a new day
So spend it how you like
And enjoy life

Kiara Brown

What is life today?
The meaning of life is life
Life is amazing

Jakayla Gordon

Japan is so fine
In the winter time is snows
The buildings get cold

Alexia Bryan

As the sun sets I
Watch as the pink sky turns black
And day becomes night

Leslie Coronado Hernandez

I went to the zoo
I saw an elephant there
Waiting to be fed

Terry Dela Cruz

The air will cool down.
Leaves will be raked together.
Autumn is coming

Malachi Ancrum

Bounce the basketball
We will be victorious
We will be awesome

Eric Churchill

As the big wind blows
The leaves on the trees fall off
The leaves blow in rows

Justin Smith

Turn the game on now
So that we can play today
So I can beat you.

Malik Fobbs

The day I wake up
I want to play some football
Time to come inside

Jahari Venning

Spring is in the air
Flowers are growing sky high
People like the weather

Leticia Velasco

Seasons change all year
Winter, Fall, Summer and Spring
There are four in all

Syncere Washington

It is cold outside
The bears are hibernating
I need chocolate

Angela Ramirez Arreola

Chilly day and night
Leaves dancing in the cold air
Bright stars in the sky

Rachel Easterling

Everything around me,
Calling my name Jane,
All around lockers,

Jessica Estevez

Cherry blossoms so delicate and fragile
Pure white or the lightest pink
Called Sakura in Japanese

Sarah Douglas

Shafts of light who webs
of dew where spiders saunter;
sometimes we miss it.

Slumber comes easy,
soothed by summer hum of
insects still awake.

Dusk welcomes the cold.
Over mountains I come from,
a light fog descends.

This sticky season
only whets air, as earth thirsts,
waits, patient for rain.

Cold brown grass cradles
the body; snow falls slow on
frozen grey feathers.

If bud breaks open,
it awakes, begins life again,
then I, too, can bloom.

Light seeps slow, surrounds
me, all things, this morning: we
belong to the dawn.

2 Plays

Defeated Knight

Jahari Venning
J'Niyah Long
A'Lanna Ellison
Nadia Polite
Jessica Estevez

CHARACTERS: Jahari- King, J' Niyah- Knight, Alonna Serts- Nadia,
Noble- Jessica
CONFLICT: The Knights can't decide who is the best

KNIGHT ONE: No, I'm the best knight though, you
bee headed clack-dish.

KNIGHT TWO: How dare you insult me thou yeasty fool
boin horn beast.

KNIGHT ONE: Just admitted I'm the gets cut off.

KING: What is all the commotion.

KNIGHT TWO: She thinks she is the best knight.

NOBEL: King J, is there anything you need me to do?

KING: No, Jessica I got this go get the presents.

NOBEL: Yes sir. (walks away)

PEASANTS: Sir, did you need me.

KING: Yea, wassup go get me something to eat.

PEASANTS: Wassup cuz

NOBEL: I'm going to follow her.

KNIGHT TWO: Sir, if you wanted something to eat. I could have got it to you, know I'm better than her.

KNIGHT ONE: Because I am thou... (gets interrupted)

KING: That is enough, both of you are very great Knights, so I don't know why y'all are. Arguing or fussing this comes to an end now.

KNIGHT TWO: King J is right, we should put this to a end.

KNIGHT TWO: Yes, we should put this to an end I'm sorry.

KNIGHT ONE: I'm sorry, too.

PEASANT: That is so cute.

KING: Where is my food.

PEASANT: Right here sir.

NOBLE: Its freshly prepared.

KING: I rarely say this but thank you.

PEASANT: You're welcome.

NOBEL: Now that everybody has solved their problems, how bout we all have a dinner together.

PEASANT: Including me?

KING: Including you!

The End

Vikings and Peasants

Jahari Venning
J'Niyah Long
Nadia Polite

CHARACTERS: *Ted the serf, Victor the Viking, Mike the knight, Jessabelle the noble, Alex the king.*
CONFLICTS: *The Vikings are trying to take all our peasants and money. Before or after the bubonic plague.*

JESSABELLE: yes your highness, I do think that the

MIKE: Hey hey hey hey cut that conversation now, the Vikings are attacking and taking the peasants with them!

ALEX: oh this shall not do!

JESSABELLE: whatever shall we do sir?

MIKE: what we must.

ALEX: and that is?

ALEX: oh you boil-brained bum Bailey, just go into town and protect the serfs.

MIKE: yes your majesty.

JESSABELLE: and what exactly are we going to do?

ALEX: give them what they want.

JESSABELLE: *gasp*

TED: you goatish flap mouthed foot licker unband me.

VICTOR: shut your frothy common kissing fustilarian mouth; and you give me all your crops and money.

MIKE: *grabs his hand* not gonna happen.

TED: *goes to get the king and noble*.

TED: your majesty, there is a battle going on in the village.

JESSABELLE: this shall not do.

ALEX: let me grab my bow and arrow.

VICTOR: give me all your potatoes, corn everything.

TED: never.

VICTOR: then you leave me no choice.

TED: *frightened*.

VICTOR: *goes to slay him but gets a bow and arrow to the shoulder.*

MIKE: there's something on your face.

ALEX: are you ok?

MIKE: I eat pears, pears from Paris

The End

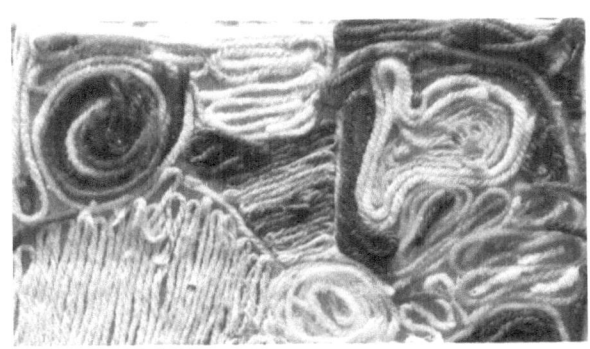

During the Black Death

Alexis Fielding Williams
Antonio Payton
Jesus Merida
Lucio Lisanti
Damon Jones

KNIGHT: (the noble walks in) The king is dying, the king is dying. What shall we do?

NOBLE: We shall command the serf to give us the medicine, it won't be a question it shall be done

NOBLE: (walk to the serf) Hey you artless hell-hated foot licker give us the most fine medicine you have!!!

SERF: And why should I give it to you

NOBLE: Because the king is dying

SERF: So what does that have to do with me? He treated me and all the peasants poorly, matter of a fact, he treated us like hell-hated scuts

KNIGHT: Give us the medicine you worthless fen sucked scut

SERF: You shall insult me all you want but the medicine has a price

NOBLE: Ok fine, I will give you an acre of land and full protection, NOW GIVE US THE MEDICINE

KNIGHT: We need to hurry, we don't have much time. We better get there before the death comes

SERF: Fine, now give him exactly two mm of this and trust he will be fine

NARRATOR: As they rush back to the castle they find there king nearly dying

KING: I need medicine now! (cough, cough)

NARRATOR: The noble handed the king the medicine

KING: (gulp, gulp) Well I hope this works

NARRATOR: A day passed and the knight and the noble came in the king's room to find a surprise

KNIGHT and NOBLE: (gasp) The has died (both bow to the king)

NOBLE: That medicine that scut gave is it might have been poison

KNIGHT: What do you mean?

NOBLE: As in he tricked us

KNIGHT: Then LETS GO GET HIM (walk to the surf)

NOBLE: You killed the king NOW YOU MUST PAY !!!

KNIGHT, KING, NOBLE and PEASANT: Ring around the rosies, a pocket full of posies, ashes ashes, we all fall down.

The End

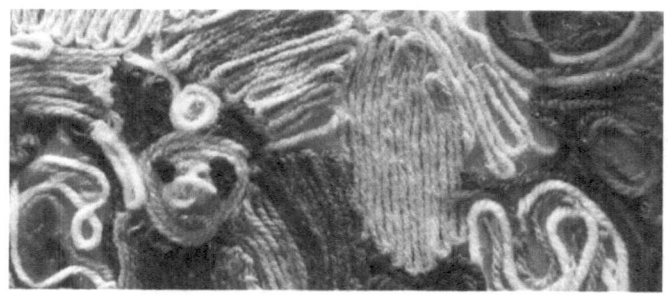

Who?

Matthew K. Greene

In the forest of Idaho was a school. A school of tall thick gates.
Trapped inside were 15 people. Five 6th graders. Five 8th graders.
Five adults.

6th Graders
Adam: the new kid
Memo: the wild one
Indie: the cheater
Dilgo: the strange swimmer
Mathel: the smart one

8th Graders
Jojo: the jock
Misty: the girlfriend
Mel: the lover
Jinkins: the best friend
Karmen: the daughter of the lawyer

Adults
Dr. Green: the mean teacher
Ms. El Paso: the know it all
Nora: the lunch lady
Principal Diesel: the nice one
Coach Candler: the tough coach

They were confused. Karmen thought Mathel was the one setting this trap thing up. Karmen told Dilgo about it. Dilgo agreed.

They all found a box in the cafeteria, It said, "Take the yellow hall passes to the rooms you will be staying at until the last two" in typed letters. It also said, "Last one in their room will be eliminated."

Coach Chandler freaked out because he did not know what eliminated meant. He grabbed his pass, Jojo's pass and Jojo (the best football player). He began to run.

Principal Diesel tried to calm them down and keep them all together but they went away.

Principal Diesel gave up to grab his pass and walked slowly to his room. He became the first one to get to his room and became first place.

Coach Chandler became second place ditching Jojo behind.

Jojo eventually found his room (3rd place).

Indie's room was right next to Adam's so she just followed Adam. She wanted the easy way. She rushed in quickly. 4th place.

Adam became 5th place.

Mrs. El Paso told Nora and Dr. Green that the Principal was faking. She said it could be Diesel doing this game. Nora did not believe her because she had known Diesel for a long time. The adults would want to confront Diesel later.

Dr. Green: 6th place

Mrs. El Paso: 7th place

Nora: 8th place

Mel, Misty and Jinkins the popular kids found their rooms:
Mel became 9th place, Misty became 10th place and
Jinkins became 11th place.

Becoming 12th place by rushing and being confused was
Memo.

Meanwhile Karmen and Dilgo stalled Mathel so he could be
last. They felt if he was last he would not eliminate himself
and would admit.

Dilgo was 13th place and Karmen was 14th place. Making
Mathel last.

LATE AT NIGHT:

The Mystery person planned. Planned gas (carbon dioxide
gas) in his room. Mathel coughed and gasped while trying
to escape. Mathel was eliminated.

Adam, Memo, Dilgo, Indie
Jojo, Mel, Misty, Jinkins, Karmen
Dr. Green, Mrs. El Paso, Nora, Coach Chandler, Principal
Diesel

They found Mathel's dead body, head down on a desk.
Dilgo despised Karmen, Karmen was in shock.

The Adults (Dr. Green and Mrs. El Paso) told Coach Chandler. They became tired trying to find ways to get out the building. They were stuck. They couldn't find things to break the thick glass windows.

The next game: four corners. Four gas cans. The number four killed Mathel. The safety number was four.

Coach chandler the usual, he rushed to put his can (#3) at the recording closet.

Everyone stayed to guess or think. Everyone picked up the #4 and was safe.

A dark voice on the speaker said Coach Chandler would be the next one eliminated. Coach Chandler threatened Diesel not to put a finger on him.

The mysterious person planned, planned and did the day after. High hot temperature, venom, and the neck. Coach Chandler was eliminated.

Adam, Memo, Dilgo, Indie
Jojo, Mel, Misty, Jinkins, Karmen
Dr. Green, Mrs. El Paso, Nora, Principal Diesel

A note lay on top of the body. "There is a sleeping snake under this table, in a cage. Wear the metal glove. Each of you will tap it on the head. If you awaken it you are dead."

One by one they tapped the sleeping python on the head. There soon was two left, Indie and Adam. Indie put cold water on her glove because she heard cold water only calms snakes.

She put water then tapped it. The snake awoke and tried

to attack Indie. She removed her hand quickly. Adam did not have to try. Indie ran away.

That afternoon came. Everyone was separate. Indie received a note on the small TV in her room. "Go downstairs, room 127 for safety."

She ran down. She stood in the room alone in front of the thick glass window.

The mysterious person planned by buying a golden arrow. The mysterious person released the arrow into Indie's heart. Indie fell.

Adam, Memo, Dilgo
Jojo, Mel, Misty, Jinkins, Karmen
Dr. Green, Mrs. El Paso, Nora, Principal Diesel

The remaining heard a crash. The arrow was still inside Indie.

THE NIGHT GAME:

Dilgo was eliminated. He was eliminated by the killer's choice. He screamed & was in rage. He was mad at Karmen. Dilgo had a rampage.

Everyone felt it was unfair. Mrs. El Paso looked at Diesel. Diesel said he had nothing to do with it but Dr. Green did not believe him. Nora still believed Diesel was not the one. She thought it was a child.

Mrs. El Paso set up a midnight watch. Everyone ended

up sleeping. Dilgo stayed up because he was terrified. He went for a swim.

The mysterious person awoke and followed him. Dilgo swam. The mysterious person replaced the bleach with acid. Dilgo's flesh melted away slowly. Dilgo was eliminated.

Adam, Memo
Jojo, Misty, Mel, Jinkins, Karmen
Dr. Green, Mrs. El Paso, Nora, Principal Diesel

They woke up to find Dilgo missing. They followed the blue tape on the floor, that led them to the swimming pool.

Jinkin stopped Jojo from going into the pool trying to save him. It was acid.

The next game was the temptation game. Each of them were tested, each denied the temptation but one.

The mysterious person planned and stabbed Principal Diesel in the back. Draining all his blood out. He lied in a coffin never to be seen again till the last three. Diesel was eliminated.

Adam, Memo
Jojo, Misty, Mel, Jinkins, Karmen
Dr. Green, Mrs.El Paso, Nora

Mrs. El Paso did not think Diesel was dead. Nora told them (Plus Dr. Green) Diesel was dead and one of the children (one of them) planned it. Mrs. El Paso still did not believe Diesel was dead.

There was a dig that coffin up game. Nora and Mrs. El

Paso was left. Mrs. El Paso was last and dug up the coffin that said eliminated.

Mrs. El Paso locked herself in her room. She took all the scissors in the school because she knew you could open the school doors with scissors. Little did she know, a penny or any coin could also open the doors.

The mysterious person unlocked her door with a penny. She used the arrow the killer used for the death of Indie. Mrs. El Paso pleaded and begged for her life to be spared as she walked backwards towards the window. She had somehow managed to open the window with a scissor.

The killer was about to release the arrow. Instead Mrs. El Paso fell out of the window killing herself. Mrs. El Paso was eliminated.

Adam, Memo
Jojo, Misty, Mel, Jinkins, Karmen
Dr. Green, Nora

The mysterious person was sick of Nora's horrible cooking. The killer put toxic dose on the ice cream when Nora had went away. Nora ate it slowly, Nora was eliminated. Her head fell in the ice cream, in front of the rest.

Adam, Memo
Jojo, Misty, Mel, Jinkins, Karmen
Dr. Green

Mel and Jinkins went into a room making out. Mel was Misty's boyfriend, Jinkins was Misty's best friends/girlfriend. They found a dead while kissing, It was a janitor's body. A janitor? They looked at him dead on the floor. Soon they were both knocked out by a mysterious person.

They were put into the computer lab posing as dolls in suits doing business work. A dose put within them making their muscles weak. They were sleeping inside but to them they were dead. They vanished away from the lab.

Seven hours later the dose begun to wear off. But most of their muscles were weakened. When awoken he broke away from his doll poses. Sliding on the floor to try and get the school phone. Jinkins woke to see Mel on the floor.

She wanted him to get the phone on the faraway desk. He got the phone and she pressed 9. Misty came in black clothing. "Look at my boyfriend trying to call 9-1-1."

Mel: "Miszy." (Her mouth muscles were weak.)

Misty: "Be quiet! You cheated on me, Mel. How do you think I feel? You were my lover. And you were my best friend, Jinkins." (Still pointing the gun at Mel)

Jinkins: "Dauhnt Mishy."

Misty shot Jinkins dead.

Mel: "Sowwy Missy" (his mouth muscles were weak as well) "I luff you."

Misty: "Then why did you cheat on me? I loved you." She looked at him. "You are eliminated." She shot him in the heart and ran out as fast as she could.

Misty was the killer.

WHO?: PART 2

6th: Adam, Memo
8th: Jojo, Misty, Karmen
Adults: Dr. Green

Misty: "I couldn't have done this without you."

The other Mysterious person: " I know but.. So we have to talk about payment."

Misty: "I just paid you $10,000 I stole from my dad's case. How am I suppose to pay you more?"

The Other Mysterious Person: "Well I need another 10,000 by tomorrow or I will expose you."

Misty: "Ok. Ok. So who's next."

The Other Mysterious Person: "Dr. Green."

Dr. Green was threatened to go outside. He took the keys left in his room. He took the bus putting on his belt. The other mysterious person used a remote to control the bus. Dr. Green crashed into the thick gates. Dr Green was eliminated.

Left: Adam, Jojo, Misty, Memo, Karmen

Misty called The Other Mysterious Person into the forest boundaries. Misty backstabbed The Other Mysterious before he/she could tell anyone she was the killer. The Other Mysterious Person was eliminated.

Who was The Other Mysterious Person: Adam? Jojo? Misty? Memo? Karmen?

Adam had been scared from the beginning. Memo had played each game with speed. Jojo had been careful with who he spoke to. Karmen was careful with who she accused.

THE CAMP OUT GAME:

There would be a cold frost the upcoming night. For the first time they were outside. They were sent to the school forest boundaries. On the other killers coat on the back was a note in purple glause. "You could not have possibly thought the killer did it by his/herself, I helped. I Memo helped".

Left: Adam, Jojo, Misty, Karmen

The note: "Race into the forest to find your camping bags. There is only three."

They ran. Misty obviously found her camping bags with all of her materials first.

Misty: First place

Jojo rush to find his in a bush.

Jojo: Second place

Adam and Karmen began to climb a tree. The last bag was high in a tree. Karmen fell down at the last stretch.

Adam: Third place

They toasted marshmallows. They all stared at each other.

Jojo and Misty were brother and sister so they did not suspect each other.

It started snowing. They went inside their tents leaving Karmen behind. Whoever helped Karmen would die.

Jojo did not care. He took Karmen into his tent. Jojo warmed her up.

They all awoke. They began to walk back inside. Misty was shocked that Karmen was still alive. Jojo, Misty and Karmen had a talk. Jojo accused Adam of killing all those people along with Memo. Karmen did not want to jump to conclusions.

Jojo had gotten mad and chased Adam. Karmen calmed Jojo down. Jojo still had some frustration inside. He went outside to play with his football to cool off.

Misty was honest. Whoever helped last place would die. Jojo threw the football up and down. Without knowing there was a gun inside the football. With enough pressure the gun would shoot. Jojo was already mad enough. He squeezed the football on the field. Shot himself in the head. Jojo was eliminated.

Left: Adam, Misty, Karmen

HOURS LATER:

Misty pretended to cry when they found Jojo's dead body. Karmen now thought Adam did it. But there was something suspicious about Misty's tears. Were they fake?

The next day was the last day. Two people would live, the recorded speaker announced. The killer and the winner would live.

Waking up they all found a note. It was a clue. They were to do a treasure hunt. Last place would be eliminated.

Adam's clue: Who died in the forest?
            You will find the next clue.

Misty's clue: Who died in the water?
            You will find the next clue.

Karmen's clue: Who died in the gas?
            You will find the next clue.

Adam immediately went to the forest. He was now in first place.

Next clue: Memo's note, "Go where the wheels on the bus went round and round."

Misty found Dilgo's clue.

Next clue: Dilgo's note, "Go where she had an arrow of a chance."

Karmen was in last place so far.

Next clue: Mathels note, "Go find the one who was blown away."

She ran to the field.

Next clue: Jojo's clue, "Snake don't want none unless you got blood, Hun."

Karmen ran to find Indie. When she got there, there was no clue. She was getting behind.

Misty had already taken...

Indie's clue: "Go where Karmen was supposed to die."

ROUND 2: INTERCEPTION ROUND

Adam found...

Dr. Greens clue: "You've made it to the interception round. Go get the clue where it got toxic with flavor."

Karmen finally found...

Coach chandlers clue: "You've made it to interception round. Go to the clue where it got toxic with flavor.

Misty found...

Karmen's clue: "You've made it to interception round. Go to the clue where it got toxic with flavor."

They all went to the Cafeteria. There were about 40 ice cream bowls on each table. There were 12 tables. 480 ice cream bowls.

The next clue was on a banner:

"Be Careful. You can eat if you choose to."

There was a pattern that had to be followed. No one memorized the type of ice cream Nora ate. Not even Misty remembered.

Memo planned and set this part of the scavenger hunt.

Memo had put the clue deep within the type of ice cream Nora ate. Three vanillas on the bottom, two chocolate over that clue deep within the type of ice cream Nora ate. Vanillas on the bottom, two chocolate over that, three strawberry over it and a cherry on top. This ice cream would give the next clue.

They did not dare eat the ice creams. They dug into the bowls to find the clues.

Three vanillas, one strawberry. Four chocolates, and two vanillas. One vanilla and three strawberries.

Adam remembered that there was a cherry. In the cafeteria there was about many with cherries on top. One stood out the most. It looked like it was made with care. It was the best ice cream pyramid. Three vanillas, two chocolates, one strawberry, and a cherry on top.

Adam was hungry. He ate the ice cream with his bare hands. Misty and Karmen were grossed out by him. They kept digging for the next clue.

Soon he saw a tiny white card. He looked back at the two with his mouth covered with ice cream. He took the card and put it beneath his sweater and ran out pretending as if he was going to throw up.

Adam opened the card.

The next clue: "Into the lab for two."

He went to the computer lab where Mel and Jinkins died.

Adam noticed they weren't in their same positions as they were in before.

There was two envelopes. One on Jinkins blood and the other next to the telephone Mel tried to use. The room stunk. He took the one next to the telephone.

"Underneath is where he was buried. He was on top and now is underneath."

Misty was done digging because it messed up her nails. That's when she found the white card.

She ran out. She didn't read the clue yet.

Karmen saw her running with it. She followed her for she didn't want to be last. Karma went into the pitch black janitors room.

A knife was shot at her but she dodged it. Misty in the dark. Karen grabbed the knife out the wall and threw it at her. Karmen missed.

Misty jumped at her trying to choke her. They rolled, Karmen was almost out of air until she kicked her legs up. She grabbed Misty and banged her head over and over on the glass case. The glass crashed,scraping Misty's face.

"Don't... ever... hurt... any-one!"Karmen yelled at her. Misty punched her. Misty tried running away but Karmen grabbed her legs only to wrestle her.

Misty kicked her gut, giving her time to grab the knife. She was gasping. Karmen emerged, flipping to dodge the knife. Karmen threw it at her, Misty cart wheeled.

Misty threw it as Karmen back flipped. Misty ducked as Karmen threw. Misty had enough. She threw the knife hard deep into the plugger.

Karmen grasped the knife. She shook. She she was electrified. Her body began to give up. Misty walked out the room broad. Her bloody red hair dangled behind her. Karmen was eliminated.

Adam and Misty

Adam wanted to know what hid in the other envelope. He opened the envelope covered with blood. Stop cheating Adam.

Adam went to the basement. He found a. Off in. He opened it to find principle diesels pale body. Above the casket it said the last clue.

" in honor of my death. Go to locker 15"

A small piece of paper was what PD held. Adam grabbed the paper. It said the word. " mystery."

Time was running out. Adam went to locker 15. He unlocked it with 1.2 and 3. He found an lfox tablet within the locker. He turned it on. The tablet needed a password. He put in mystery. Mystery was denied.

Adam pronounced mystery thinking he misspelled it. "mystery. Mystery. Missy. Misery. Missouri. Mystery?" Misty passed by misty. "misty." Password was accepted.

3 Poems

About Halloween

What Is Halloween?

Jaelyn Gadsden

What is Halloween?
Is it a time to celebrate?
Is it time to give ?
Is it time to look back on the old days?

Halloween is a day where you be yourself.
Watch scary movies
Hang with friends
Receive or give candy
Or Party

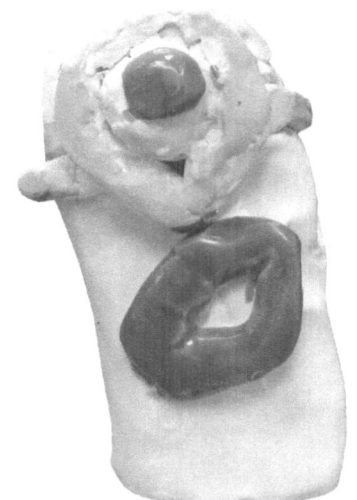

But the next day
Mom is checking bags
Candy disappearing
Tummies hurting
Mouths aching

But think is there a bad side?
Where is the fun?
Are we too old?

Halloween isn't everything
You think and hope.

I Hate Halloween

Erica Stoker

I see things that are not there.
Every day I can never tell the difference between
Reality and simply my imagination.
Voices always stuffed to the back of my head;
Am I expanding my mind, or am I just going insane?

Every Halloween people dress up like monsters.
Through the year I see enough monsters
Linked to the back of my head;
Made into reality by my troubled eyes.

I hate Halloween.

I hate my body, so why on earth
Would I gorge myself with sugar?

Oh, yes young children and their candy.

Teenagers and their parties.

Me connected by skin to the
threads of my bed sheets;
Mind glued to horrid memories.

Am I expanding my mind or
am I just going insane?

I hate Halloween.

Anything Can Happen

Kyliah Catalan

The thrill of the night,
horror fills your ears,
dark and dreadful,
you can't see a thing.

You think you're fine in the dark,
but you're not,
something so horrifying is coming toward you,
but you don't know.

Anything can happen
on this terrifying night
that no one knows.

There are blood sucking things
looking for a snack,
things creeping and crawling
all around
that could eat you up
and kill you,
things that will haunt you until your scared to death.

Beware what you see,
never go out on this horrifying night,
everything evil comes out
possesses you
until you're dead.

You never know
what's coming,
but beware.

Anything can happen on Halloween night.

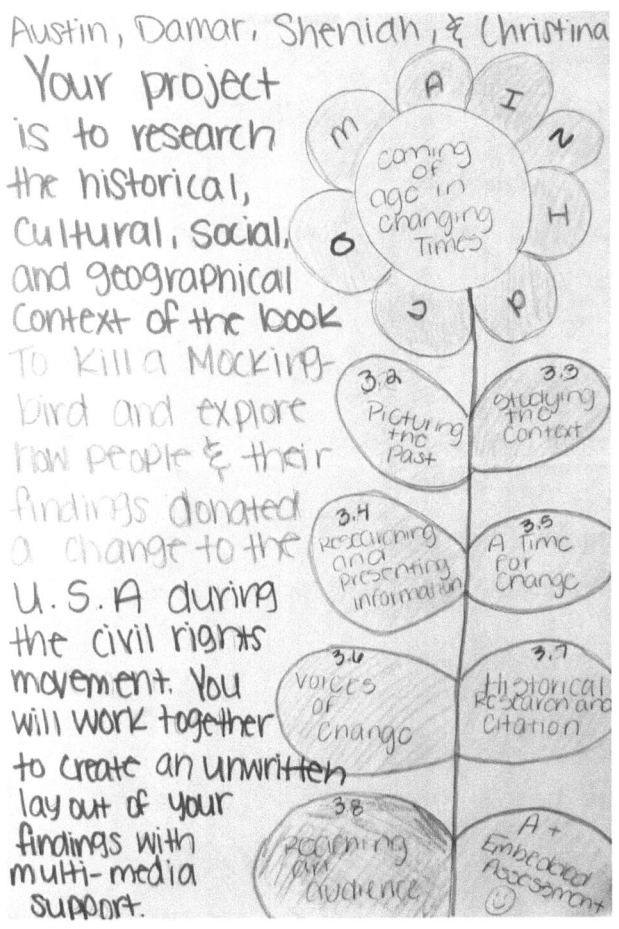

Austin, Damar, Sheniah, & Christina

Your project is to research the historical, cultural, social, and geographical context of the book To Kill a Mockingbird and explore how people & their findings donated a change to the U.S.A during the civil rights movement. You will work together to create an unwritten lay out of your findings with multi-media support.

Every Night And Day

Kayla R. Cannady

A chilling feeling rushed through me
As I sat on my bed.
The air was thin and eerie.
I tried to convince myself
It was all in my head.

I was filled with panic and fear
I knew something wasn't right
As I turned to look at my window
I saw a creature there in plain sight.

It's features were dull
But it looked at me with dead cold eyes.
At the same time
it started to observe me
I remained calm to my surprise

The creature seemed all to familiar
As if we made contact before
Then I started to wonder
What is this creature looking for?

No words were spoken
No sounds were made
I'm still left wondering its motives
As it visits me now every night and day.

Tonight Is The Night

Taniah German

Tonight is the night
To have a great fright
Lanterns burn
Bright yellow light
While the moon shines bright.

Darkness comes to make it night
Children are given a spooky fright
Witches fill the sky
ON broomsticks way up high

Black cats race witches
While wizards wands begins to twitches
Ghost and goblins join the fun too
Flying around and shouting BOO!

Trick or Treaters playing tricks
On all those who didn't give them sweets
Everyone's excitedly scared
While pumpkins relax and give evil glares.

Don't be surprised nor scared
Just be prepared
'Cuz tonight's the night
To have a great fright.

But Now, As A Ghost...

Karisma Hamilton

Fresh out of school,
While the air is cool.
Kids run straight home,
To put on costumes made out of foam.

They run out into night,
All with smiles on their faces.
Trying to go door to door,
Acting like they're running races.

Me and my friends,
Are daredevil teens.
We like kicking in pumpkins,
And hearing kids scream.

We decided on one house,
That we saw one night.
To see if someone would make it,
Without running with all their might.

I was scared to death,
As the unlucky loser was me.
But it was too late,
As I saw my sister flee.

The monster pulled me in,
And made my nightmares come true.
But now as a ghost,
I'll haunt people like he would too.

I Don't Do Poems

Jasmine Sanders

Trick or Treat
Smell my feet
Give me something
Good to eat.

Trick or Treat
Ghost and Goblins
Witches and vampires
But where's the goodies??

Trick or Treat
Kids say
doors open
scares in the atmosphere.

Trick or Treat
Zombies coming alive
Witches flying on brooms
Spirits comes full moon rises

Trick or Treat
All you hear
Like a song that will
Never leave your head

Trick or Treat
Smell my feet
Give me something
Good to eat.

I don't do poems

On Holidays and Christmas

Have A Good Night

Zaviera Brown

As a silent sleeping night,
You can see in the windows light.
Though the snow flakes fall form the sky,
You start to know its Christmas night.

Ho ho Santa Claus says,
I can hear the reindeer's above my bed.
Sound of the foot prints inside my house.
You can hear all the giggle sounds.

Christmas morning everyone's awake.
It's time to open presents on a wonderful day.
As you smell the food it's a good delight.
Merry Christmas and have a good night.

Christmas O' Christmas

Briashmel Bell

Christmas O' Christmas what a happy time of year
Children can't wait to see what Santa has brought
Families sing with love and cheer
Have I been naughty or nice? Is their only thought

Tis the meaning of Christmas, the meaning of the season
Mary gave birth in a barn, the Messiah was born
Jesus Christ is his name he's the real reason
We must remember this as we eat our turkey, rice, and corn

The sales are always after Christmas but no one knows why
20% off 10% off says the signs
The stores are jammed with raging customers
who look as if they are going to die
But they really do not care as long as they get inside

Kids all over are happy Hooray no school they yell
But teachers still give them packets of homework
Geesh no sympathy at all.
It's winter break.

And we don't want to do homework.
I mean can't you tell?
They know that they must do it or else
Their grades will really fall.

I Don't Want Anything For Christmas

Kayla R. Cannady

Sitting by the campfire
Illuminating the backyard with its light.
Its blazing flames keep me warm
In the freezing cold winter night.

I sit outside isolated from everybody
While they all socialize together,
Raving about their fancy gifts
And keeping warm from the cold weather.

I didn't want anything for Christmas
I didn't yearn for material things like others
I just wished for peace to be instilled and for joy to be there
Upon my friends, sisters, and brothers.

While everyone inside shows off what they got
And their materials, I watch their faces glow
But as they only gain temporary happiness
I accept whatever I already own
and the true happiness I know.

Not Feeling It

Solomon Adams

The time of Christmas can be great and filled with luck,
But for many others, like me, this time of year can really
suck.
I know that what I'm saying may sound crazy to you,
But I promise I will force you to you see my point of view.

There are lots of bad singing carolers croaking bad verses,
And crazy men on the street corners selling knock off purses.
The smoke fills the air from fires that are ignited,
And various family members show up to your home unin-
vited.

Your parents make you wear large coats
and put you in a bundle,
and when you step inside the mall, the isles are like a jungle.
There are kids that throw snow balls and scream and yell,
and taunt.
Then there are itchy ugly sweaters
that were knitted by your aunt.

People seem happy and they
Scream with glee and cheer,
But I personally can wait
Until next year.

A New Year Will Begin

Kamron Washington

Christmas cheer with my family all around me here and there.
We gather around laugh and smile and talk about our lives.
Kids stare down the tree ready for their presents.
We play games inside and out.
Everyone is ready for the day of gifts to come about.

Relatives we haven't seen in a while come down and hang out.
We smile and we laugh,
We hug and we cry the ones that we missed.
Those are the moments that we would always miss.

The day was getting closer and closer.
Everyone is ready for the day to come.
Drinking eggnog all together making people smile and snicker.
The kids are ready and are urging for the presents

The day is here everyone is screaming in cheer.
We open the presents and take picture of the reaction.
We never want the day to end.
We love this day and we are sad it has to end,
But a new year will begin.

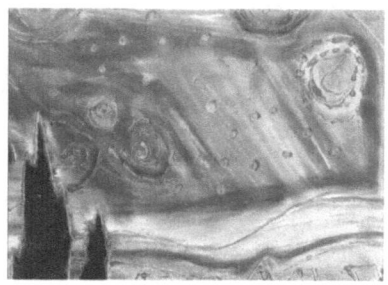

Which Holiday?

Kyliah Catalan

Lights everywhere,
Singing and love,
People showing love,
And giving.
Smiles all around,
And happiness through out the town,
Celebrating the birth of Jesus.
Oh Christmas, a beautiful cheer.

But what about New Years,
Cheering and parties,
Resolutions and love,
Something new,
Something better,
Say goodbye to 2014,
And have a good cheer to 2015,
Count down to the day,
And see the ball drop
In New York City.

If had choose which day,
Well I wouldn't know what to say,
Because they're both
Wonderful holidays.

Joy

Caitlin McCants

Christmas is here It's full of lots of cheers,
Wrapping paper all over the house,
Bags flying everywhere.

Baking Christmas cookies
With warm milk on the table,
Just sitting around laughing
While enjoying Christmas cheer.

It's time to wake up and unwrap all those presents.
Being happy & thanking everyone for that nice
Christmas gift.
Christmas is the best time to spread
Joy.

Christmas Was Here

Anauticah Fulton

Christmas was here
Everbody was filled with cheer
Santa brought toys
For every girl and boy.

The new year is almost here
And I'm ready to change my ways
So this year wouldn't get slayed.

Birthdays are coming
And other holidays too,
Bring the laughter
And spirit too.

Have a good time
With family and friends.
Never letting
The fun end!

Real Christmas Poem

Harvey Hamilton

snowball is white,
blood is blue,
frost bites kill,
or the flu.

snowman frozen in place,
children yelling,
heard from space,
blankets and snow shoes.

wounderful tones,
lots of balloons,
family, even the dog
is happy too!

doesn't make sense to some,
but that just means
you're too ignorant
to try to understand.

RAVEN BAILEY

Christmas Musings

Karisma Hamilton

It's literally the night before Christmas,
And homework is a curse.
And starting to talk to people more,
Is just becoming worse.

I am sitting here thinking,
How would it be at school.
And then I think of Christmas,
And realize I'm a fool.

Gifts and jolly spirit,
And laughs fill the air.
I look around and see smiles,
And happy children everywhere.

Christmas is a great time,
I love every part of it.
And I hope everyone,
Has a really good bit.

Christmas Cheer

Hannah Garcia

Children smiling while adults laugh
The little gifts under their oh so bright Christmas tree
Little toy trains and Christmas movies on the move
Oh, don't you feel the groove

Christmas is here!
Christmas is here!
The little children cheer
All around the town are flashy lights
Oh, don't you feel their delight

The sound of those bells ring their ears
While people sing those Christmas cheers
Everyone's happy, everyone's smiling
Don't you love when Christmas is around?

Even if you're sad, even if you're mad,
The Christmas cheer is never that bad.
So come on now,
Time to spread the Christmas cheer.

Thinking About The Holiday

Mackenzie Cook

Christmas.
Snow
Break
presents
shopping
Santa
trees.
These things and many more come to mind when thinking
about the holiday.
However is that what it is really about?
You don't need them to have a great holiday.
All you truly need is the people you love.
They will spread enough joy and happiness
for the rest of the whole year.
What would Christmas be like spent alone?
You could still have these things but alone,
Christmas is not the same

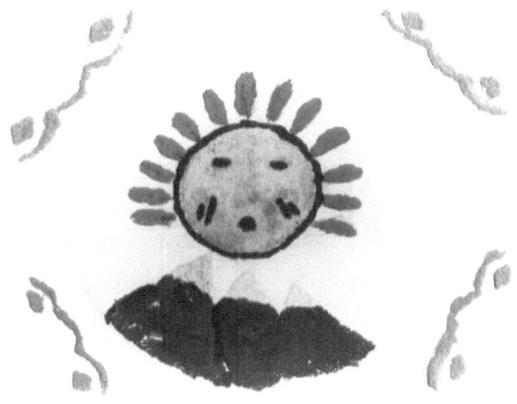

Christmas

Jasmine Sanders

Christmas
oh Christmas
you are here
Santa is coming
so bring the cheer

wrapping paper
oh wrapping paper
is this true
no wonder if your parents is always in the room

we think
oh we think
when we were young
we believed that Santa
is real but where's the
evidence

Christmas tree
oh Christmas tree
where were you
these days

Christmas is here
the best of the year
too bad
that it have to go
for the very next year

For the presents,
thank you one and for all.
the big ones many thanks,
And fewer for the small.

bye Christmas
oh bye Felicia
out with the old
and in with the new

this year was great
time for the new
Christmas is gone
but wait 364 for it
again

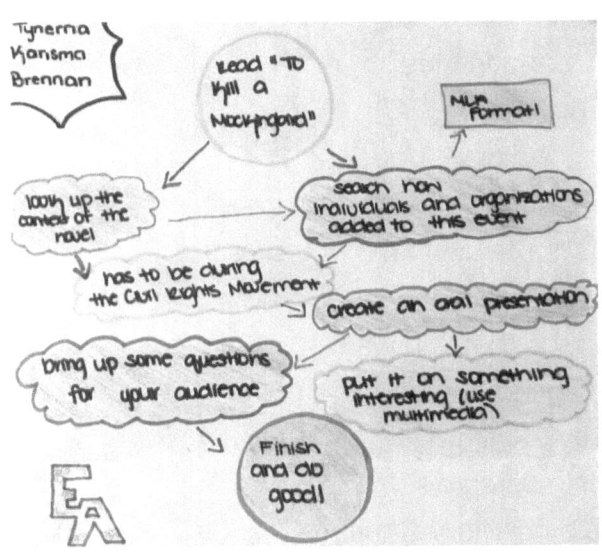

Ho Ho Ho

Jemar Jones

Snow is white and trees are green
When you hear the sound Ho Ho Ho
That means the big red guy just put
a present under the Christmas tree

Santa is coming to town and
he's gonna check his list not once but twice
So you better hope your good because
Santa always knows who been naughty or nice

Sitting In The Living Room

Kayla Belk

Sitting in the living room
With family and friends
Opening up gifts
And eating the great good food
Seeing everyone is the best thing ever
Christmas is the best time of the year
You get a lot of gifts
A lot of things that you want
You get to grind egg nog
And set my the fire
Sing Christmas carols
And have a holly jolly Christmas

Christmas

Solomon Adams

The time of Christmas can be great and filled with luck, but for many others, like me, this time of year can really suck. I know that what I'm saying may sound crazy to you, but I promise I will force you to you see my point of view. There are lots of bad singing carolers croaking bad verses, and crazy men on the street corners selling knock off purses. The smoke fills the air from fires that are ignited, and various family members show up to your home uninvited. Your parents make you wear large coats and put you in a bundle, and when you step inside the mall, the isles are like a jungle. There are kids that throw snow balls and, scream, yell, and taunt. Then there are itchy ugly sweaters that were knitted by your aunt. People seem happy and they scream with glee and cheer, but I personally can wait til next year.

From and For the Teenage Heart

Dear Love

Ty'Celia Young

He was the love of my presence,
I am Death,
And he is Life,

We had a couple of dates,
And then we stopped,
Just because he got all google-ly eyes,

Now I only see him, while I'm killing
The useless idiot humanoids,
My man never to love me again,

How dare he cry out to Happiness,
Instead of me,
The traitor who broke my soul,

How dare he,
With his baby face,
And long brown hair,

I will kiss Happiness,
She will die for what she did

Wanting it Back

Armani Mack

Young and Full of Life
Small and Innocent
Young & Fierce
Happy and Careless

Growing and Glorious
So Fly I was
Drama Less
Little Chick
Big Bright Smile
Shined better than the sun

Full of laughs
Never a single unhappy tear
Always happy and full of joy
2 parents instead of 1
Hmm had it all taken within a blink of an eye
The life of being a toddler

The Unknown

Armani Mack

I just don't know
The deep dark secrets of my past
Haunts me like, it was all just then a blast
Now it's all just a part of the part
It all just unfolded so fast
That was my very last
My only asked
I never knew what the memory hold
A painful dark mast
So thankfully its all passed
Free of the night at last
Never wanted to remember the vast moment
It was suppose to be enjoyment
Wondering if it the night was so pointless
It was all just worthless

Because of You

Armani Mack

I whined
I cried
Then choked
Red face
I woke

It was all because of you
I smiled
I laughed
I mugged
Then the whole cycle repeated
All because of you

You smiled then laughed
And blush
Wondering when I will laugh
Hmm you just never knew
It was all just because of you.

I'm Just Small

Armani Mack

Louder than a football stadium
I'm loud
Older than 9,999,999,990 million
I'm just old
Smarter than the Internet
I'm just a genius
Laugh more than clowns and the law allows
I'm fun
Oreo at times
I'm just crazy
Scarier than a bat
Over think every little thing
I'm a girl the size of a bean
Couldn't get any smaller
The truth defines me.

I'm just small.

Who Are You Really?

Jaelyn Gadsen

Are you someone that I can look up to
Look for when things are hard
Believe in to keep a secret
Know that you will trade?

At times I don't believe that's you
You always laugh when I really need you
Traded on me when I told you the deepest secrets
And talked about me when I wasn't around

But yet, I still was still your friend
I thought you would change
And go back to the old you
Always letting things go

Then I think
You aren't who I thought you were
You're no good for me
Time for you to go
Let you do you
Because I can't take it

It's not going to work
I'm a strong minded person
I can make it
I don't need you
I can do all that by myself

Mexico

Kevin Ramirez

Mexico.
Cartels everywhere, Texas from Mexico,
Drugs coming in and out.
By land, water, underground, and air.

Mexico.
Zetas doing the dirty work.
Blood splattering everywhere,
Always have their 1911 colt 45,
customized with gold and diamonds.

Mexico.
Zetas started at a young age,
Have no mercy,
They're well trained,
They kidnap and murder.

Mexico.
The president of Mexico,
Government and police have no power.
The cartels have bought it.
There is no type of government.

Mexico.
The citizens fighting in large groups,
They have weapons.
They are trained for the unexpected,
And ready to receive gun fire.

Mexico.
There is no type of government,
Police and president, so what is Mexico of?
Mexico is hopeless.
What will the future of Mexico be?

Broken Man

By Aaron McClaurine

He was a man... a broken man.
He lost his brother.
He lost his sister.
He had no wife.

He got fired.
He got rehired.
He found love.
He found happiness.

He loved life.
He sometimes hated life.
He wanted to succeed.
He did succeed.

He had lived his life.
He was eternally happy.
He had wanted to die.
He then wanted to cry.

Lonely

Kevin Ramirez

Lonely.
Have no friends or family.
Away from civilization.
Always miserable.

Lonely.
Always hiding behind the shadows.
Looking at its on reflection.
Lives in its own world.

Lonely.
Always depressed,
Crying in the inside,
Isolated from humanity.
Lonely.

I'm Lost

Kevin Ramirez

I'm lost, in the middle of the desert.
The Rays of the sun are burning against my neck.
My body is weak and dehydrated.
I found a big huge tree, with lots of shade.
I take the rest of the day there.

I woke and saw my very red skin,
Like a mandrills nose.
This happened because I was getting over tanned.
My mouth was very dry.
I thought I was going to die.

When I noticed a herd of rabbits going in one direction,
I've followed them for three hours.
My feet were killing me.
The herd of rabbits ended up in a cave with fresh water.
But the water was acid, and I drank it anyway.
I was slowly dying in a huge amount of pain.
After a few minutes later, I've started to close my eyes.
Couldn't open them again.

Criminals, Criminals, Criminals

Kevin Ramirez

There I was. Sitting down. On the porch.
Seeing people who can't afford a Porsche.
But can sure buy alcohol. And drugs.
It's getting late. And here comes the bugs.

It's 12:00 a.m., gun shots fired. Across houses.
Women still walking around. With ripped up blouses.
Children hanging around with criminals.
The criminals acting like animals.

Its dawn. Everything is quiet. And still.
Bodies are everywhere. And bags filled with pills.
The police and ambulance came, and arrested people.
And took the dead ones.
The DEA came, and confiscated all the guns.

There I was. Sitting. Down. On the porch.
Seeing how my life is influenced by criminals.
Being surrounded with thugs and crack heads.
Criminals. Criminals. Criminals.
Everywhere.

Oh No!

E. J. Hilden

Oh no!
My shoes aren't cool
And my shirt isn't cool
And my hair doesn't rock.

Oh no!
My girlfriend is not
A movie star
Or a teevee star
Or a rock star
And I am not
Justin Bieber.

Oh no!
I don't have the most money
Or the best jewelry
Or the biggest house
Or those beats headphones
Or the latest iPad
Or a limitless credit card
With which to wine and dine
Kate Winslet

Oh no!
Nothing is perfect it's all normal
And there is so much to consider
When you gaze into a mirror
And see that you are normal

And just like everyone else
With the same needs and fears
And wants and likes and dislikes
And it all drives you insane
Until you let go
Of what all of those other clowns
Think.

It Hurts

Jasmine McFadden

To see you with another girl,
That makes me just want to break down and cry.
Can't you see I'm in pain?
I told you I was trying to get over you,
You said you don't want me to.
I'm confused and don't know what to do.
I've fallen madly in love.
Every time I see you, I fall in love again.
Deep inside I get butterflies when I talk to you.
Will the torment ever end?
I think we should remain friends,
But that would add to the pain.

By: Jennifer
Jopez
6th

Cinderella walked on broken glass

Aurora let a whole lifetime pass

Belle fell in love with a hideous beast

Jasmine married a common thief

Ariel walked on land for love

Snow white barely escaped a knife

Because love means facing your biggest fears

6th Grade

My Mystery Boy

Janica
Smith

The way his skin feels
and all his complexion

The way he stares at me
with his affection

The way he smell's
like a rose

The way he see's a camera
and just has to
pose

The way he make's my
stomach feel

The way he see's right through
me to see what's real

The way he is fragile
like a toy

That's what totally make's
him my mystery boy

She Wanted Me To Break It

Lexi Bryan

She wanted me to break it
The shell I've hidden in
She wanted me to break it
So I could be free

She wanted me to say it
The words hidden from years of resentment
She wanted that blunt, funny girl
To come out

She wanted me to sing it
The songs I prayed to sing
So sweet and pure and happy
A song that was truly me

She wanted me to break it
To finally be me
To finally be free
So here I am

Kitten Snores

E. J. Hilden

I love that sometimes you're there
When I get home
And I see your smile, the glint in your eye
And I feel safe and warm
And protected from the storm.

I love that you laugh at gross things
And say gross things
And act goofy and immature
Because it is good to be a kid again
And it's never too late to have a happy childhood.

I love that you have little kitten snores
That massage the dark
And keep me from being alone
That keep me safe.

I love that you sit in the dark with me
While demons wreak havoc on my head
With patient understanding,
Never with judgment or cruelty
Waiting for the battle to end,
To be won.

I love that my bed smells like you
Soft and flowery, a gentle perfume
And that you reach out in the dark
With the most
Gentle
Touch.

That's O.K.

Jasmine McFadden

Tears rolling down my face
As you're not with me every day.
I wish I could take her place,
But I never could with my ugly face.
You always go back and forth
Between me and every other girl.
To me, you are the world,
Yet, you're torn between me and the other girl.
Every day you say you love me
Don't you see how much I love you? Don't you see?
I guess you and I weren't meant to be.
That's O.K.; I have plenty more fish in my sea.

Sometimes...

Jasmine McFadden

Love is a beautiful thing,
But sometimes it can be deadly.
I wish that you'd love me
The way you do in the messages.
I feel like I've been played
And I feel like such a fool.
Am I just your flirting tool?
Sometimes, you make me hate you...
Then again, when I see your smile,
And you trying to take a quick peek at me,
I feel like a beautiful somebody and
You make me feel special.
Sometimes, you make me love you...

Love, or So I Thought

Jasmine McFadden

In love with me.

That's what I thought you were.

Then you turned your back on me.

You had hurt me, deserted me, and left my heart to burn.

You are blinder than Adetomyrma Bressleri.

Oh, wait. You're too idiotic to know that word.

I thought without you, there would be no me.

I see now how that is absurd.

I can't believe how I made everything else blurred.

All because of those things you made me believe.

You said the sweetest things I've ever heard.

You said you loved me and you never leave me.

WHERE ARE YOU NOW?

Taken

Jasmine McFadden

It is very hard to go through my day
Knowing that you are so in love with me.
You don't understand that I am taken
Also, I feel like you are stalking me.
Continuously and throughout my day,
I notice your eyes are always on me.
Can you please move and get out my way?
Eyeing me from the hours one to three...
You don't understand that I'm taken.
You'll try to hang me on a crooked tree.
And with my corpse you will do evil sins.
Why won't you just leave this little girl be?
Taken is what I am; can you not see?
Taken is what I am now leave me be.

Who Are You?

Jasmine McFadden

An acquaintance, friend, or something more?
Some days you want me around,
others you want me to shoo.
Having a relationship with you is such a chore.
I wonder what these childish games are
supposed to make me do.
Who are you? Please tell me.

Do you love me?
Do you love me not?
Stop messing with me.
All of your time is running out of the clock.
Who are you? Please tell me.

Some days you are always around,
Others you won't even talk to me.
We walk past each other without a sound.
You're not really who you say or seem.
Who are you? Please tell me.

Get Back Up

Jasmine McFadden

Love comes around and around.
Sometimes it may knock you down.
Don't let it leave you on the ground.
Just get back up when it knocks you down.

I know love gives people so much pain.
Young or old, in the sun rain.
If you break up, you shouldn't be ashamed.
You probably dated someone without a brain.

All their pictures you don't need to burn.
Now they are none of your concern.
Maybe one day, you will be what they yearn.
Just get back up when it knocks you down.

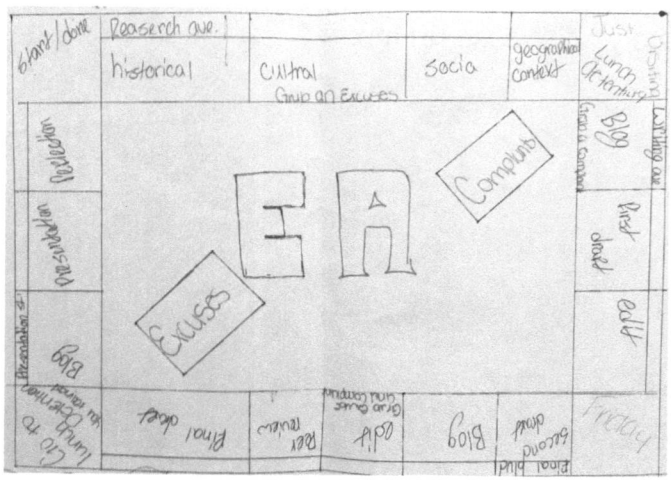

Beautiful

Jasmine McFadden

When we first met, you said everything I wanted to hear.
You always said I was beautiful,
and you always wiped my tears.
But then I started to feel used and abused.
You only wanted to party, leaving my heart bruised.

I thought that we would've made something beautiful.
But all you ended up doing was hurting my soul.
I left you to escape from your pain and wrath.
Now I'm free and capable of choosing my own path.

Not many people can say they survived abuse like I did.
I see now why it's good to stay in the place of a kid.
When we first met, you said everything a girl wants to hear.
No longer was I insecure and filled with fears.

I know that you weren't loyal or truthful,
But thanks for helping me know that I'm beautiful.

My Language

Jasmine McFadden

I thought we would make a good team.
We did everything together, we were a good couple.
Apparently, to you, that's not how it seemed.
All you do now is look.

When I try to converse, you never pay attention.
You look away and act like the invisible
I say pay attention, but you do not listen.
The way you treat me now, is not excusable.

You say that you love me, you'll never leave.
For a while I had thought that was true.
The person I was in love with, is now gone.
Now I see that this is not the real you.

Personality

Jasmine McFadden

You and I were meant to be.
You just have the best personality.
Some girls look for looks and muscles that they can cuff.
I look for somebody who cares and loves.
Thoughts get upset when these hustlers leave them.
While that's happening, I still got the same man.
Girls friend-zone the prince charming, and date the work.
Maybe if you dated the prince, one of your relationships
would last and work.
You see, him and I were meant to be.
Cause he has the sweetest personality.

A Sonnet For Students

E. J. Hilden

Shall I ask thee to follow format please?
It makes your writing easier to dig.
When all is lumped together, it's like cheese
that smells a lot and makes it look too big.

Line breaks are your friend, as are goodly rhymes
Stanzas are not to be feared but revered.
It doesn't take a whole bunch more your time
To do it right, to make your poem clear.

Redouble efforts to do just your best
A couplet is in ways the hardest thing
A quatrain is a place for eyes to rest
When words to rhyme to soul you choose to bring.

Writing sonnets challenge your every whim
but lumped in blocks they seem so very dim.

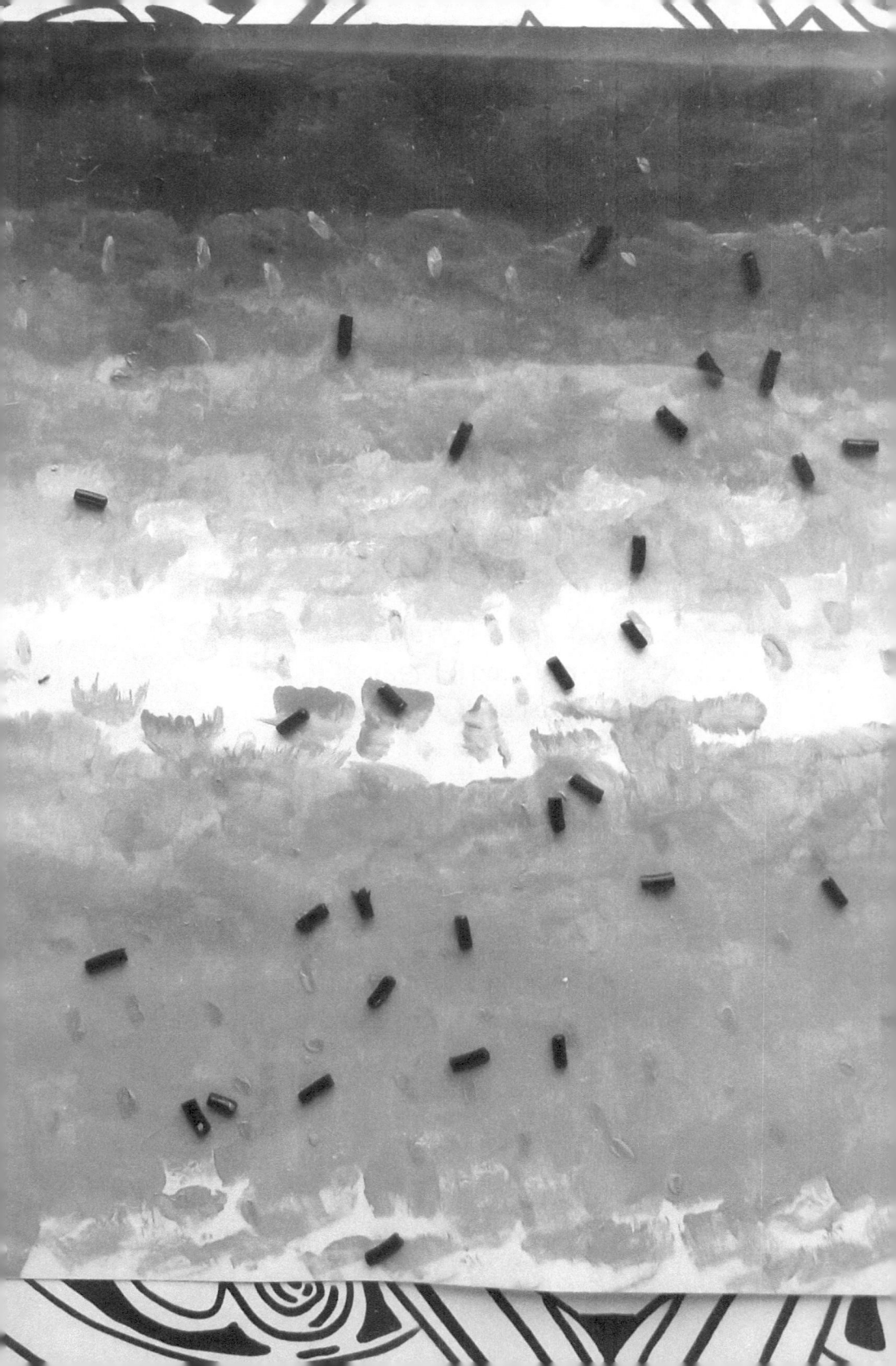

4 Short Stories

Forever Alone

Jose Orellana

A freak, a monster, a psycho, that's what they called me. Just for being different, for having a gift I never wanted, for being able to do things nobody else could. The ability to see the supernatural.

You must understand that I have always had the gift, I was just somehow born with it. Since them I have seen creatures of the dark, creatures of the light, ghosts, ghouls, but nothing had ever terrified me as much as the spirit I saw on Halloween a few years ago. My name is Daniel, and this is the story of how I died.

I was just finishing my cheap vampire costume, putting on the vampire teeth and cape. I grabbed my pillow case, put my earphones and phone in my pocket, and headed out of the house. As usual, nobody greeted me as I got out of the house. Even my family hated me for being strange.

One of the only friends I had was this girl. She some- how could sense spirits. Not see them as clearly as me but sense them. As I walked out, she hurried to my side and greeted me with a hello. I replied in kind. We were sort of silent, after all, Halloween is when most of the ghosts are out.

We soon saw a house and hurried to it. I knocked and said Trick or treat. A short bald man came out, and dropped a long object in my pillowcase. It was a tooth- brush. Out of all the freaking things he could give us it had to be a toothbrush. When I looked up he laughed like crazy and slammed the door in our faces.

I sighed and continued from house to house. Those times we were lucky. My pillowcase was over filling with Twix, Snickers, and a bunch of other stuff. I was feeling so epic, nobody had ever given me much candy before. That's when I noticed something.

There were no spirits anywhere, even though this was supposed to be when they were most free.'

Suddenly, I felt something strange, as if somebody was watching me. I turned slowly and looked down the street to Old Mary. It was one of the oldest houses here, and it was abandoned. Many companies had tried to destroy it, but they never could, because every person died before they could make a scratch to it.

`I looked clearly, and I don't know how, but I could see the window from far. I saw a pair of eyes, blank as the snow and a smile that stretched from ear to ear. I forgot how to breathe. Everything seemed to dim and the only thing I could see was the thing. Out of the blue, it appeared to be ten feet from me. That's when I saw it.

Its skin was pale, and it was wearing a dress. It towered over me and I started to shake, I couldn't even say anything. My breathing was coming in gasps. It opened its wide mouth and started to yell. DANIEL!!!DANIEL!!! I covered my ears and was yelling, its scream was in my head!!

I was starting to cry. I felt like I was crazy and wanted it to stop!!

Suddenly it stopped. I looked up saw my friend. She had a worried look. Then I realized that I was on the floor. I got up and noticed that everyone was looking at me, even the adults. I stood up and everybody looked away.

Then she hugged me and said "I sensed it too, whatever that thing is, it wants you."

I agreed and started to walk home, and she went back to her home. I was looking down the whole time, too busy thinking to see the person ahead of me. I bumped into him and heard "watch it punk." I started to turn away but it was too late.

They had already surrounded me. The bullies, they would beat anybody up for even the smallest thing.

"Hey ghost boy, too busy talking to your dead girlfriend to see me." They all howled in laughter. Then it got serious.

I saw it before I felt it. I landed on the floor, cringing at my cheek where he had punched me. Then they all started to kick me, laughing all the time. Every hit brought a fresh wave of pain. It was excruciating. I was too pained to notice they had stopped. They whispered to each other rapidly they all agreed on something. I could scarcely make

out what they were saying"Throw.......Old Mary...
Lock him in.."

They roughly lifted me, and started to carry me. I tried
to fight back, not because I was scared of the house, but
of what was in. Soon we arrived. The house was 3 stories
tall, with almost no windows except for the one in the front.
Its black towers were despairing, with already faded paint.
They kicked the door open and threw me in. I tried to run
out but they closed it and held the door closed.

Then it was only me in the dark house.....alone. I yelled
with all my might, but nobody heard, the house was very
far from the town. I could hear them laughing. Then I heard
a moan. I froze, and found our that it was from outside.
I had the feeling that alerted me if something supernatural was near. All of a sudden I heard screams, the bullies' scream. I could hear ripping, liquid splattering onto
the ground, and then silence. A dark liquid was seeping
through my door, and I clearly knew what it was.

I slowly began to open the door. I looked on the floor
and there was nothing. That's when I felt it. I felt a drop
fall on my shoulder, I looked up to the sky and saw that it
all was all red and raining blood. I ran through the streets,
finally glad to be out of Old Mary, but terrified to see all this
blood. The houses were not there. The town was not there.
Everything was gone. I looked desperately around but
there was nothing.

Suddenly forms began to rise from the blood. Taking shape of humans and beings made of blood. Their
mouths open in an endless moan. The blood was soaking
my shoes, and started to be at my ankle. The only place to

be safe seemed the house. I started to wade to the house when I was pulled under. I fought to get up but the blood was like a heavy blanket.

My lungs were screaming for air!! I could hear voices saying "Help me, kill him!!" I burst out of the blood and climbed to the steps of the house. I was soaked completely in blood. I opened the door and slammed it shut. I sank down and closed my eyes. When I opened them I was dry. I looked outside and there was the town.

Slowly, I realized that it had not been real. It had all started when I tried to get out of the house. Something wanted me in here. I slowly got up and looked around. I stopped, because that thing was right in front of me. I had stopped breathing. I could hear my heartbeat in my ears.

"WHAT DO YOU WANT!?!" It looked at me and cocked its head.

"Some fun," it replied with a smile. I turned and ran, my feet slamming against the floor. I could hear it chasing me, so close that I could feel its breath on my neck. It pounced on me, forcing me to the floor. It raised its hand with talons instead of nails. I screamed with fear, trying to get it off. It swiped at me and everything went black.

I woke up strangely with energy. I sat up and groggily wiped my eyes.

"Daniel" said a girls voice. I looked around and realized that it had come from downstairs. I walked down the steps to the door. Somebody was hammering the door down. The door opened and my friend and cops got in.

"Hey" I started to say but then the strangest thing happened. They passed right through me. I gripped my chest, feeling where they went through me. I began to feel horrified. I was dead. I walked out the door. And saw 4 body bags with scientists examining them...the bullies.

They could not see me. They all passed me.

This is my journal that I have written in my room. My family occasionally comes up to see what that writing sound is but I don't worry, they will never see me. There are things out there that people cannot fight, things that humanity cannot comprehend, and things that science can't explain. It has been two years since my death. I don't know how much this is going to last. But for now, with nobody to be with me, I will be forever alone.

Charlie Kennedy

Mackenzie Cook

I dressed up for the huge Halloween party that everyone from my school was going to. I was going as Dorothy
from the wizard of oz. I'll admit, my costume was kind of
lame but oh well. No one really dresses up for Halloween
anymore. I checked my phone, seeing if my friends were
here to pick me up yet. There were no new messages.

Sighing, I walked down stairs and then the lights
went out. I screamed loudly and rushed outside. Something jumped out of the bushes as soon as I ran out, and
screamed. It was my friends in full costume. They almost
gave me a heart attack. Everyone laughed while I tried to
calm down. Then we were off the party.

When we got to the address, it was a huge house in a
fancy neighborhood.

"Wow" I said in amazement. This had to have been the
biggest, most expensive house I've ever seen.

"Who's house is this?" I asked. Luke, who was
dressed up as a super hero, explained that it was Destiny's
(the most popular girl in school) house. It figures it would
be, her family was rich.

We got out of Calum's car, and immediately my friends
Lloyd and Chloe ran up to me and hugged me.

"Charlie! You're finally here!"

We all walked inside to the party. Everyone was
dressed up in various colors and costumes, and then there
were the people who didn't put any effort into their costumes at all. Many girls were wearing black and had cat

whiskers painted on their face. That must be the popular costume this year.

There was a large table with a lot of candy and loud music playing throughout the house. It was well decorated and I have to admit, I was impressed. I talked to different people that I knew from school and took selfies. It was pretty fun.

After about an hour and a half, Ashton, Calum, Luke, Michael, Lloyd, Chloe, and Destiny all walked up to me.

"Hey Charlie, we are going to the murder house! Wanna come with?"

The murder house? Have they lost their minds? The murder house was an abandoned house half way around the town from where we were now. Apparently, every person that moved in died. And there were rumors that on Halloween night, the spirits of all that have passed came and took you with them. I am gullible, but I had a weird feeling about it. It wasn't a good idea and rumors aside, I didn't want to get in trouble for trespassing.

"Oh come on Charlie, you can't actually believe those old stories." Said Ashton.

After a lot of peer pressure, my friends finally convinced me. So we drove the short way to the old house. As we got out of the car, I felt chills. This place was creepy. I didn't want to be anywhere near it. The paint was chipped and falling off of the house. The shutters were lightly banging against the house. We all slowly approached the door and with a light nudge, it opened with a creak. I peeked inside and all I saw was old, dusty furniture.

We pulled out our phones and used the flashlight

feature. We entered the house. We started walking around the bottom floor and found nothing. However, we heard strange noises. The whole group was terrified, including me. We started for the door but before we could escape, the door slammed shut with a loud bang.

"I told you guys we shouldn't have came! Now we are gonna die!" I shrieked. There were noises coming down the stairs and Calum, Michael, and Ashton were trying to get the door open. The noises got louder as the rest of us tried to find another way out. I heard someone scream. It sounded like one of the boys.

I turned off my flashlight, terrified. I ran under the dining room table in the house. I stayed there for a little while, hearing the screams of my friends. I wanted to help but I knew there was nothing I could do. I took a deep breath and screamed when I felt someone touch my shoulder. I turned to see a white face. The man that died here.

"I have your friends. You can either leave or join them," he said.

I knew the obvious choice was to join them and try to save them. I loved my friends. I loved my life more though. I told him my choice.

"You actually thought you could get out that easy." He laughed to himself.

"Please just let me go!" I cried.

I wish I could say that I had actually managed to escape. I wish I could say it was a prank. I wish I could say I saved my friends. I wish I could say none of it had ever happened. My name is Charlie Kennedy and I have been in the Murder house for ninety six years.

The Dutchman

Alicia Alexandrea White

What is Halloween? Halloween is when you can dress up. Put on a costume that isn't you. When you dress up, you want to scare people or just for fun, put on makeup and trick or treat around your neighborhood. Halloween is a special day for some people. For instance, me.

My birthday is on Halloween. It is good and bad. The good reason is that I turn a year older every year on that day. The bad reason is because a lot of people call me the "Devil Child." I don't know why but they do.

Most people have fun and some don't. Mostly because they get scared and when they get scared, their day gets bad because they don't like getting scared. If you want to dress up on Halloween, go right a head. I really don't know why you would. Everybody is telling you to just be yourself.

Well on Halloween it is always different. When you go trick or treating, you are pretending to be someone your not. You can be yourself on Halloween and still have fun. You can be the artistic you and still be with your friends and still scare other people.

I've heard people say, that everyday on Halloween, a devil child is born. I mean like, if you know its not true, then don't say stuff like that.

One cold winter night, early in the New Year, a certain Dutchman left the tavern in Tarrytown and started walking to his home in the hollow nearby. His path led next to the old Sleepy Hollow cemetery where a headless Hessian soldier was buried. At midnight, the Dutchman came within site of the graveyard. The weather had warmed up during the week, and the snow was almost gone from the road.

It was a dark night with no moon, and the only light came from his lantern. The Dutchman was nervous about passing the graveyard, remembering the rumors of a galloping ghost that he had heard at the tavern. He stumbled along, humming to himself to keep up his courage.

Suddenly, his eye was caught by a light rising from the ground in the cemetery. He stopped, his heart pounding in fear. Before his startled eyes, a white mist burst forth from an unmarked grave and formed into a large horse carrying a headless rider.

The Dutchman let out a terrible scream as the horse leapt toward him at a full gallop. He took to his heels, running as fast as he could, making for the bridge since he knew that ghosts and evil spirits did not care to cross running water. He stumbled suddenly and fell, rolling off the road into a melting patch of snow.

The headless rider thundered past him, and the man got a second look at the headless ghost. It was wearing a Hessian commander's uniform. The Dutchman waited a good hour after the ghost disappeared before crawling out of the bushes and making his way home.

After fortifying himself with schnapps, the Dutchman told his wife about the ghost.

By noon of the next day, the story was all over Tarrytown. The good Dutch folk were divided in their opinions. Some thought that the ghost must be roaming the roads at night in search of its head. Others claimed that the Hessian soldier rose from the grave to lead the Hessian soldiers in a charge up nearby Chatterton Hill, not knowing that the hill had already been taken by the British. Whatever the reason, the Headless Horseman continues to roam the roads near Tarrytown on dark nights from that day on.

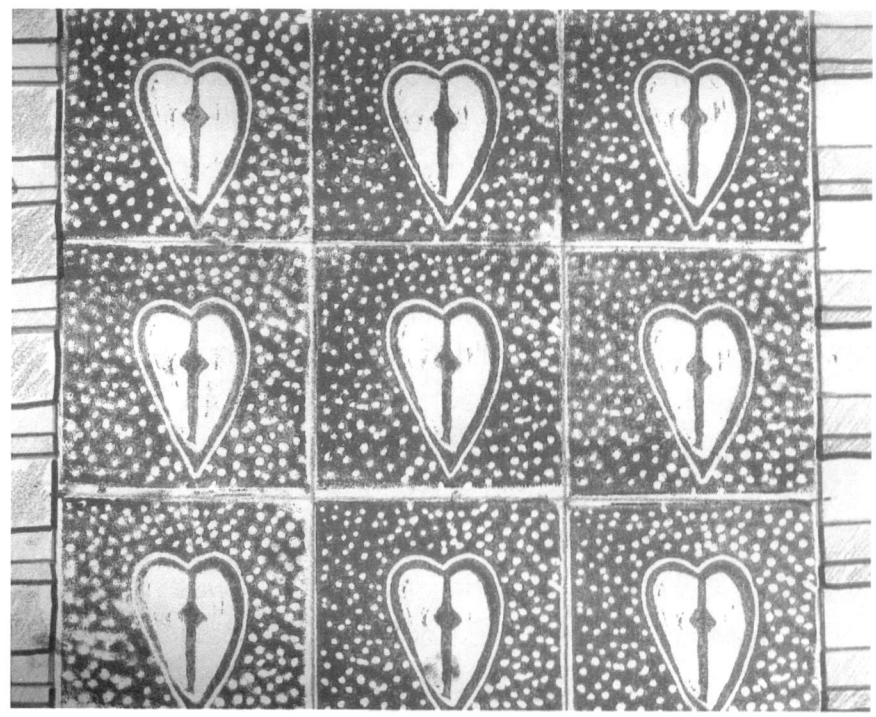

The Door

Andrew Brown

The evening was cool and slightly foggy. My night before Halloween was just what you would expect from a teenage boy. I sat around in my room, watched TV, ate, and planned where I would go and what I would do the next night. But there was one thing that I couldn't get off my mind. It was a year ago, on this same night. It still bothers me to this day even though it was a year ago when it happened.

It was around ten o'clock at night when the incident was said to have taken place. I saw it in a news report the on Halloween when I went into the living room to ask my parents when we were going to leave the house. Apparently, the police sent an officer out to the local cemetery around midnight to make sure that nobody was doing anything stupid out there. What I heard after that shocked me. The report said that when the officer arrived at the cemetery, he noticed a peculiarly strong smell as soon as he stepped out of his vehicle. He said that as he stepped closer to the gates, the smell kept getting stronger. He was just going by the moonlight at that point, so he couldn't really see anything strange.

But when he pulled out his flashlight, a horrendous sight shocked him straight to the core. On the gates to the cemetery were two bodies in different states of decomposition, speared through their backs by the fence. When he got back to his cruiser, he radioed in and asked for a forensics team to investigate the bodies. They said that the two people were obviously dead for a while, so they sent another team out to search the cemetery for any signs of what happened and how they got onto the fence. The other team reported back saying that there were two graves that were dug up and emptied on opposite sides of the cemetery. One of the two bodies belonged to a man named Benjamin Wand, and the other two a woman named Beth Shapiro. That's when I didn't want to hear any more and went back up to my room to try and forget what I just heard. I didn't think anybody I know was related to them, so I tried not to worry about it. But since tonight is the anniversary of the unsolved crime, it was all coming back to me.

The next night, Halloween, I had already put my costume on and was about to head out the door to meet up with my friends. It was a simple costume, just a soldier's uniform. It only took about two minutes to put on.

One of my friends, Tom, texted me to tell me he was out of the house. As soon as I replied to his text telling him that I was about to come out too, I went into the dining room and told my mom that I was heading out. She told me to be careful and that she loved me, all the things that you would expect.

When I was halfway out the door, though, as if reading my mind she told me,"Oh, Al. Don't go to that grave yard. Okay? Do you remember what happened last year?" I simply nodded and closed the door behind me as I walked outside into the refreshing breeze of the autumn night.

After about five minutes of walking, I reached the cluster of trees in Tom's neighborhood that he told our group to meet at. But just what I expected, Tom was out of sight. I looked up into one of the trees and of coarse, Tom was sitting on one of the higher, more concealed branches.

I yelled up at him,"I see you Thomas!" He then jumped from branch to branch as he descended the tree until he was finally at a good height to jump without hurting himself.

"How'd you see me ,Al?"

I looked at him like he was stupid."Tom, you always climb that tree when we come to your neighborhood. And by the way, where's Red and Jacob?"

As if on cue, Jacob stepped through the bushes and walked over towards us.

"Where's Red?" I asked.

He pointed over at his house. "He's still in the bath-room, putting in the details on his face." He must have seen the confused look on my face and explained,"He's supposed to look like a complete psychotic murderer and he's putting a lot of detail into his makeup."

I just shook my head and Tom commented with,"He always overdoes his makeup on Halloween. But I guess it is still pretty cool how he can make it look like his flesh is peeling off." Jacob and I nodded in agreement.

We waited about half an hour until Red finally stepped out the door and started down the street to join us. We all just stared at him with disappointment. I really expected his outfit to actually look real and terrifying. But no, it looked like he tried to rush on his makeup and just smeared a lot of fake blood on his self. We tried not to bug him about. He did at least try. But our focus went from him to Tom in just a matter of seconds.

"Alright guys, as you know from all the previous Halloweens that we were unsupervised, I am the glorious planner and coordinator for this wonderfully a-mazing night. So, what I have planned for us is simple. We go to every house in the neighborhood with trash-bags and get as much candy as possible. but we're gonna do something different tonight. Something that would have been unthinkable last year. We, my friends, are going to that cemetery. Remember, the one where the... incident happened?"

Even now, a year after the incident happened, I'm still afraid and paranoid about that cemetery. It's hard to believe that Tom actually wants to go to that cemetery.

"Tom, you can't be serious," I said to him.

He turned his head to look at Red and Jacob,"You're still afraid of that place? It's been a year. Nothing's gonna happen."

I tried to convince him that this wasn't a good idea. He didn't listen. He just kept saying that there was nothing to be afraid of now, and that the thing with the bodies happened a year ago. There was absolutely nothing I could say to stop him from going. And I sure wasn't going to let him go by his self. I had no choice but to go with him.

When we were about twenty yards away from the cemetery gate, Jacob stopped dead in his tracks.

"Guys," he mumbled. We turned towards him. He kept pointing at something on the ground beside him. I couldn't see what it was, so I stepped beside him and looked at the ground where he was pointing. What I saw disgusted me. There was a cat on the ground. Dead and mutilated.

Its nose was cut off and there was a deep slice from a knife going along its throat. Its fur was matted to its side with dry blood and there were ants crawling up its legs. When I finally locked away, Tom and Red were next to me. I never noticed them move. I was distracted by this bloody sight. Tom seemed perfectly content despite what he was seeing on the ground in front of him.

"Come on, guys. Don't pay any attention to it. Let's just keep moving," he said. I didn't have any problem with that. I just wanted to get away from what I was seeing.

When we reached the cemetery gate, I could see flashlight beams moving through the graves. Tom and Jacob pressed their backs against the posts of the fence. Red ducked behind the sign about ten feet away from them. I just laid down in a bush. I looked over at Tom. I could barely see him in his black jacket and pants. I now see why he chose to wear those clothes for this Halloween. The people with the flashlights were moving closer to the gates. I lowered my head back down into the leaves so that I was concealed, but I could still see with one eye. I saw one of the two people unlock the gate and push it open. It squeaked as it moved on its hinges. From where I was I could see that the two people were actually the new cemetery guards. As the second man stepped out, he just let the gate slowly close behind him on its own. When the guards were far enough away as to not hear us move, Tom moved from his position and caught the gate before it could close all the way. The rest of us moved from our hiding places and stepped through the open gate.

When Tom came through, I asked him,"So, what's the plan now?"

He wiped the sweat off his face."We're going over to that big tomb over on the north side."

I just shook my head, knowing that I couldn't argue with him. We continued walking between the graves until we reached the north side of the cemetery. "I know this thing's around here somewhere. I saw it just the other day. It was a big tomb with these two crossed spears on the fr-" Red pointed over towards a place where there were less graves, "Is that it?"

Tom looked over in the direction he was pointing,"Yeah, I think so." He started toward the tomb and Red and I reluctantly followed. Jacob walked a completely different direction.

"Jake? Where're you going?" Red said, beginning to follow him. Jacob remained silent. He was staring at something on the ground. I could feel myself beginning to tremble as I walked over to where he was standing. I honestly didn't want to see whatever was on the ground. I knew it wasn't going to be anything pretty. I was right. The thing that was on the ground this time wasn't just laid out on the ground like the cat we saw earlier. This was different. And it wasn't just some dead animal. No, it was worse. It was... a head. A human head. There were dents in the skull where the person was obviously bludgeoned to death. The nose was cut clean off and the left eye was hanging loosely out of its socket. But what I thought was the worst detail of all was the fact that the jaw had been ripped off and there was still blood dripping from the wounds.

Jacob slowly reached his trembling hand towards what little was left of the lower jaw. He stuck his finger under the steady drip of blood. "It- it's still warm." he stuttered. And I thought it couldn't get any worse. This was murder, yes. But it happened recently. Very recently. Nobody noticed. Nobody heard any screams. Not even the guards knew that this had happened. We were the first ones to know about this murder.

I threw up. There was no way to hold it back. I was sick to my stomach. I just wanted to go home. I wish that I never came to that cemetery. Especially on Halloween. I knew that something bad was going to happen. And it's going to be the same next year. And the next. And the next. This trip wasn't worth it. I don't even know why I listen to Thomas. All he does is get us in trouble. But this is a whole different story. I would give anything to just have gotten in trouble. I now wish that we had just gotten caught at the gate. But now, there's no turning back. This can't just be forgotten. I have to know what happened here or else this memory will haunt me for the rest of my life. I had to stay with Tom and the others and go along with what I got myself in to.

Tom fumbled a flashlight out of his pocket and scanned the ground around the head for any signs of where the rest of the body went. Sure enough, there was a trail of blood leading east from the head. But as Tom kept shining the flashlight at the ground, I could see that we were all standing in a gigantic puddle of blood. That was when Jacob lost his stomach. He also threw up and added to the disgusting puddle that we were currently standing in.

Without saying anything, Tom waved his hand indicating for us to follow him. I didn't hesitate. I just wanted to leave and get this over with. We continued walking until the thick trail of blood stopped and we were at the door to a different tomb.

Tom forced a smile. "I guess we're going into a tomb after all. Yeah guys?" I just glanced at him and his smile faded. He just cleared his throat and tried to open the gate of the tomb. It didn't move. "It's locked," he said, frustration evident in his voice. He kept trying harder.

"Stop Tom!" Red yelled at him.

Tom turned toward him and put his hand over Red's mouth. "Are you crazy, Red? You'll get us caught!"

"I don't care anymore, Tom! I don't care! I want to get caught! I want to get caught and get out of here. I'm not going to stay here and look into a murder that we have no reason to get involved with. If you want to stay here and get killed by whoever is doing this, then fine. They're obviously not done. Nobody can stop whoever is doing this. They're going to keep going on and on. Every Halloween, something like this is going to happen. It's happening in this one cemetery. We don't need to worry about it unless the guy who's doing this kills someone we know. I'm leaving. And there's nothing you can stay to stop me!"

Tom looked guilty. I seriously thought he was about to cry. "Fine, Red. If you want to leave, then leave. It's your decision whether you want to stay or not. I won't keep you. Go."

And with that, Red started walking away. I wanted to go with him, but I just couldn't bring myself to do it. All Tom wanted was to get through this with his friends. I couldn't take that away from him. I would be overwhelmed with guilt. It would hurt too much.

"Here," I stepped over beside him and pulled on the lock while he tried to push the gate open. The chain was rusty and seemed like it could just fall apart at any moment. I gripped the lock harder and Tom took a step back, preparing to kick. I moved to the side just in case he accidently kicked me. He kicked at the gate as hard as he could and the chain on the lock shattered. He was panting from the exertion, but still smirked as he looked into the darkness. He pulled his flashlight back out and shined it into the tomb.

There was a spiral staircase leading in the only direction possible: down. Tom stepped inside and shined his flashlight straight down into the darkness. "This goes really far down," he whispered.

Jacob finally stepped inside with us and asked," Tom, are you ever gonna go down, or am I gonna have to push you."

Tom just chuckled," Well, let's go then," and we descended into the darkness.

After a while Tom shined his flashlight down again. "Hey! I can see the bottom now!" he said happily. We kept walking until we reached the bottom. When we made it and finally planted our feet down onto the cold dirt floor, there was a single dark corridor leading to an ancient looking door. I was reluctant at first, but part of me wanted to know what was on the other side of that door. I started toward the door and Tom and Jacob followed.

I didn't notice at first, I was too distracted by the mysterious door to pay any attention to it, but there were layers upon layers of dried blood coating the floor and walls. That's when I had to take a deep breath and remember what we were dealing with here. I noticed a small object on the ground beside me and knelt down to examine it. When I saw what it actually was, I jumped back to my feet and leaned against the wall.

It was a finger. A finger off of a man's hand. That's when I decided against staying in that tomb. I was done. I started running back up the spiral staircase. I didn't care about how Tom felt at that point. I just wanted to get out of this cemetery.

When I made it outside again, I fell down into the dirt and started dry heaving. As soon as I finally regained my strength, I got back to my feet and went south towards the cemetery gates. But when I got to the trail we were on earlier, I noticed something that wasn't there before. There were four freshly dug graves with four very familiar names on them. Allen Simmons, Thomas Dean, Red Johnson, and Jacob Johnson. But there was something different about the one with Red's name on it. It was filled in. I fell to my knees, and did something that I hadn't done yet. I cried.

I never noticed when a man dressed in a dusty, blood covered suit came behind me. A hard kick to the back sent me into my own grave. And seconds later, I felt pounds after pounds of dirt thrown on top of me until I could no longer breathe and it was all over. And I now know what's behind that door.

Her Map

Matthew K. Greene

It was Fall.

Fall was the season everybody had to go back to school. The leaves fell upon this private school in South Carolina. A school where you needed not to wear uniforms. In fact it was 2020, almost all schools in the south needed no uniforms. The year 2020 was a year of the hip twist and 1920's fashion mixed with 2014 designs. They all came back to 8th grade with drama.

However Lucy had just moved to this school leaving all her friends behind in Washington.... She was quiet, alone, and down. Then she met Queene.

Queene had a past. A past of leaving friends behind to become a better fake person/poser.

Mr. Grand had a two person project for the class. The best team project would win an extra 50 points. A kid named Prince dared Queene to work with the new girl. She didn't want to because she felt that Lucy was a loner. So Prince said if she and Lucy won the extra credit then he'd give her $50 bucks he earned. And if he won then he wanted 50 bucks. If no one won then no one would get money. But Queene wanted the money for the new puffy twisty dotted 2020 skirt or duffies.

Her map:

Plan Duffie skirt Work with Lucy> Let her do all the work> Win> Get $50 bucks> Buy skirt

Queene: Hi. Are you Lucy? The new cool girl? (Faking as usual)

Lucy: Yeah?

Queene: Wanna be my teammate?

Lucy: I guess so.

They were to make a project about the changes of the decades for the nineties to the 2020's. It could be on any topic. Lucy was Mexican and Queene was African American. So they (Lucy) decided to make a board of the changes of clothing for Mexicans and African Americans over the decades featuring a celebrity for each decade. Lucy wanted to take care of the African American board.

Queene: You do the board for both. And I'll send you the info through MySpace.

Lucy: What's a MySpace? I don't have one. Don't you have Facebook?

Queene: No, so get a MySpace. Get one.

Queene had no MySpace Account. Lucy soon got a

MySpace but couldn't find Queene. Lucy made the board as they both Lucy and Queene presented. Prince and Present presented a project on the growth of America through each decade. The project was to be based on facts. Mr. Grand loved Lucy and Queene's creativity so they won, they (Lucy) included facts so it was okay.

Her map: Work with Lucy *check> Let her do all the work *check> Win*check> Get $50 bucks*check> Buy skirt

Queene was at the Mall on a Saturday with Garcia shopping for flannels and duffies. They were at the corner looking at some duffies.

Garcia: $40!! They're so expensive. Lucy had come to the mall as well and well.

Lucy: Queene? (Queene turned and then turned back)

Queene: Oh no.. Hush and don't make eye contact.

Lucy: Sup, Queene. (She stood next to her)

Queene: Hi.

Lucy: Duffies. Nice.

Garcia: When I saw these I was like, "Ha! Dumb." But if you look at it in a different angel then it's actually bomb.

(Queene stomps on her foot)

Garcia: OW!

Lucy: What just happened? (She stood in shock)

Garcia: I'm Garcia and I'm totes addicted to Flannels and Starbucks so let's go buy some. (She grabs a hold of Lucy's arm) You can join us when your foot heals, Queene.

30 minutes later:

Lucy: I gotta meet my mom at the lot. We should do this more. Hit me up, okay?

Garcia: Okay. See ya! (Smiles and waves as she goes) Why don't you like her?

Queene: She's a freakin' loner.

Garcia: She seems chill to me. Just think of her as another character in your life. Be positive. That moment Queene's mind blew up with ideas.

Her map: Project Fame Queene was known around her school but Felicia was known even more. Even Lucy knew Felicia before she knew Queene. Felicia had her two main friends, Patricia and Alicia. Queene was always one step behind Felicia. Right now her main friend was Garcia. Lucy could be her one up.
Talk to Lucy> use Lucy against Felicia till volleyball season> Stick with Garcia> By then you won't need Lucy.

Months passed by and soon enough winter came by. Snow fell. Sun pillow case feathers everywhere. Queene, Garcia, and Lucy became best of friends. They continued visiting the malls and planned for other places.

November: Volleyball Season They hid around a corner.

Lucy: So what do I do?

Garcia: That girl's weave is falling out.

Queene: Hush.

Garcia: You hush.

Queene: Anyways Lucy, Dive in ask her anything then pull her weave out, give it to me after.]

Lucy: You need it? (Sarcasm)

Queene: No, I just dare you. I bet you'll fail. $6 dollars.

Lucy: Deal.

Garcia: Count me in.

Queene: No, stay Garcia. Record it.

Garcia: Hehe (chuckles) this is gonna go viral.

Lucy walks calmly to Felicia. Felicia was talking to Patricia and Alicia.

Lucy: Hey, Felicia, mind if I take it?

Felicia: Take what?

Lucy: This! (She pulls out her weave then runs) Bye Felicia!

At Lunch: Queen's group sat together. The violet weave lied out on the table.

Felicia: Before I tear y'all up, how dare yall. (Her hair was smoothed back with water. She was there with her squad/main friends)

Queene: Is there a problem, Mystique?

Felicia flipped the table over. Clashing, pouring all the food on the floor. The people in the Cafeteria turned to look.

Felicia: Who done it? Whose idea was it?

Queene pointed at her friends like a coward.

Lucy and Garcia: What!

Alicia: So it was yall. (Queene walked away in her hills clicking while her duffies swung. She needed to stay away from drama in the public)

Lucy: It was her! (Queene walked stopped)

Queene: Yall chose to do it for the money. I don't need yall. Especially you Lucy, I only used you for my needs. Puh-leeze, like I need you. (She walked away faster) (Garcia walked away from Lucy. She gave up on Queene)

Felicia: Nahh, last time I remember, you pulled it out. Garcia and Lucy where beaten up right after school. Felicia's squad beat them up. They were not caught, and no one reported. They stayed in school without a suspension.

November 13, 2020, a day after:

Dear Queene, I can't believe you would say that to me. I mean after all we've been through. I know I could probably text you this but I choose not to. So like I was saying. I cannot say much more because I am sick of you. You made me who I am. You were my only friend when I was down all by myself. And now I know you only was using me. I do not... I ugh! Why? You know what, never mind. Queene don't text me again. Don't talk to me. Don't call me. Don't talk about me, again. Don't speak to me. Wait did I say that again? Yeah I did. I'm serious. Dueces, Lucy.

Garcia's map:

(Emptiness) Talk to Lucy *check> use Lucy against Felicia till volleyball season *check> Stick with Garcia> By then you won't need Lucy.
check December 5, 2020:

Present had always had a crush on Queene. And Garcia, Lucy and Herself would hate Present for his creepiness. But now Queene was desperate. She was low, no main friends. Felicia was coming on top once again. Felicia was now Captain of the Volleyball team. And Queene didn't make it in the team. However Garcia and Lucy did.

Present: I bought you an early Christmas present. (He put out the small black box)

Queene: Huhhh..What is it now? (She said as she polished her nails) She took it and opened it. It was big diamond ring. It said, "Will you date me?" Many things popped into her mind.

Her Map: Backup Procedure Say yes> Make people talk> Let the rumor be true> Get nominated for Queen of Hearts> Go to the Valentines dance with Present> Dump him in front of the crowd.

Queene: She smiled, "Yes." New Year's, Year 2021 February 12: Spring was here. A season where mating begins for humans. Present's feeling to Queene was: Roses are red, Violets are blue, Sugar is sweet, And so are you.

Prince: So this kid said something dump on a throwback Thursday. It was that kid who said 21 about five years ago. He still doesn't know the answer. It's funny.

Queene: (Walked with her head up) He's faking. It's a comeback method.

Prince: Wow. I never thought.

Present ran up to her, and hugged her. He kissed her on the cheeks. Queene's face was in disgust.

Present: So babe the dance is coming. Wanna be-

Queene: Of course I'll come with you. Soon enough Valentine's Day came. Present was crowned and Queene was as well crowned for Queen of Hearts. At that moment Queene broke up with Present. The crowd ohed as Present ran off crying. It was a shocking event. Garcia and Lucy shook their heads in disgrace. Queene smiled at them. Say yes*check> Make people talk*check> Let the rumor be true*check> Get nominated for Queen of Hearts*check> Go to the Valentines dance with Present*check> Dump him in front of the crowd

Queene Felecia Present wanted attention. She couldn't control her maps.

*Check after *check. So she stayed on top till the end of the year. Summer came with sunlight and the smell of melted sticky ice-creams.

One day Queene went to the mall and found Garcia and Lucy shopping for Flannels.

Queene: Hey! They tried not to pay attention but she came to them. So how are you guys.

Lucy: Fine. (Garcia stayed quite)

Queene: So how's life?

Lucy: Fine. (Garcia hushed) We gotta go.

Queene: I'm sorry! Garcia! Lucy! (She cried as they walked away faster).

Queene dropped. Another autumn came by and Queene was on top. Number one still above Felicia. Prince and Present moved. Highschool was here and Garcia and Lucy made something out of themselves. Planning for college and a better life as Queene still focused on her maps. Grades filled with F's. Once A's, now all F's.

The year 2052: She still carried her maps and made new ones for every situation she was in. She got arrested for theft, she stole the new improved Duffie. She was bailed out by Lucy. She was a successful News Caster. And Garcia became an Actor who lived in Hollywood and Queene knew it. Always seeing her ex-friends on television hurt her.

Lucy: I'm going back to Washington.

Queene: What? (In shock)

Lucy: I got a job to newscast on Seattle's Channel Five News.

Queene: You can't go. (She touched her hands. Lucy removed it slowly)

Lucy: Let me take you home. Queene: Are you gonna still hold on? (Head down) Lucy: Let me take you home.

Queene: Okay.

Queene soon got a therapist/phycologist. She told her story. The story she knows. From Lucy to Present she had maps. Her maps. She told told her every detail, exactly. The therapist did not know what to say. She had sad life with busy parents. And everything was with her maps. They never were positive. She Remembered:

Garcia: She seems chill to me. Just think of her as another character in your life. Be positive.

Queene was tired, she fell, passed out, fainted and weak.

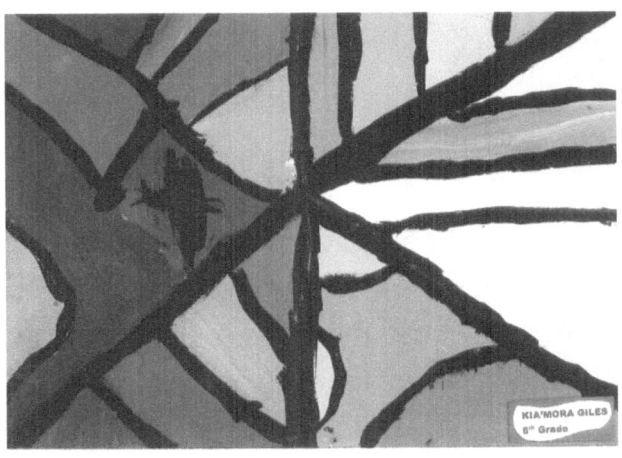

KIA'MORA GILES
8th Grade

Dear Diary

Ayleen Galvan

Dear Diary, It is Halloween. It's also the first time I've spent Halloween with any one other than myself. As you know diary, recently I've been stuffing the lost souls young girls, 13-19, and cramming them into modern bodies. They're not allowed to leave my castle and I use them for my own personal pleasures!

Bibigul (demon, 665 AD)is surprisingly good at washing dishes. I've also tried mixing them with magic. Which has gone rather well, especially for Aureole (1947), who is able control all the elements!

But enough of that, this morning stated with Penny (shape shifter, 2012) and Christie (human soul in a robot, 2012) were especially excited today. They kept asking if I'd take them out to festival or whatever.

I was about to smack them for interrupting my time with Aysel (Slime Alien), but then I really thought about and realized that don't really celebrate anything. I just sit around all day. Even before I had the girls I just lazed around and watched TV. But NO MORE. I'll ask Christie and Penny how to properly celebrate Halloween, right away! ... When I'm done with Aysel.

Dear Diary, I asked and got way to many responses. It also seems Aureole and Bibi knows what this is too. It has a lot to do with costumes, death, Satan Himself, and demanding food from strangers. Very odd. Penny told me that before this life she used to party every Halloween. I told her we cant have parties because I'm slightly xenophobic. Between you and me diary, I'm VERY xenophobic.

But then Christie told me she just sat around and watched movies. I told her she was GENIUS. I mean, that's what I do anyway, so I was all for that idea. But I soon realized that I have no idea what to watch, and that scary movies weren't my forte. Ironic, isn't it?

Dear Diary, No one here knows how to rent a movie. Expect Christie. And no one here knows what "Blockbuster" is. Except Christie. The problem is I can't send a robot in a schoolgirl outfit outside. I don't want to go outside. And no one else is allowed to really go outside. .... Okay, you got it out of me, diary, there are two girls that I allow to go out, Beline and Lebine (belly-dancing twins, unknown year) . They were the soul I messed with, so I never would have guessed that if I left them out once they would become world renowned dancers.

Oops.

Lebine is hanging around today, which is probably the longest I've seen her without her twin. She looks empty and hallow without Beline. And I'm sure Beline feels the same. But I still have to talk to her.

Dear Diary, Lebine agreed to go, happy to do something. I gave her the list Christie came up with and she left. Now we wait, diary.

Dear Diary, it's 11:00 pm. I gathered the whole crew to watch the movie I was the most interested in. The Exorcist 1 and 2. Aureole immediately gasped when the movie started saying, she never saw a film in color. Which is weird because the TV is always on.

But throughout the whole movie, Lamya (Unknown) and Bibi kept looking at me and laughing like maniacs. I also heard Bibi murmur something about doing the same thing to a young boy a while ago. …. I don't want to be around either of them anymore.

Dear Diary, Needless to say, Aysel (Slime Alien) left to her room five minutes into the Exorcist, before anything that bad was happening, saying she couldn't handle the tension. Christie then suggested we watch something less intense after this then.

So I choose "Saw." I showed her the cover before we started and Aysel threw up. I didn't exactly know what to do, because it was hard to tell what was vomit and what was her body.

Dear Diary, Aysel went to sleep for the night. I feel a little bad, I didn't know she was so squeamish. I'll make it up to her.

Dear Diary, We've gone through half the list, it is now 1 AM, we're now watching Painted Skin: The Resurrection. Everyone's fallen asleep, except Lamya, I don't know If I mentioned this before, but Lamya doesn't talk. Ever.

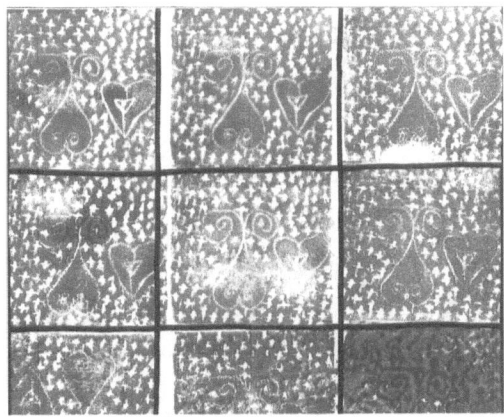

Never Will She Give Up

Angie Solis

Rose had a perfect life. For her, of course. Best mom and dad and little sister. Yet did she know it was about to change?

Woke up one morning. Frightened. Heard a gun shot. Than a loud scream. It was only 3:00 am Runs to her sisters room. Hides of course. Slowly falls asleep with her. Trying to forget. Hears sirens. Notices that her dad isn't here anymore. Curious what had happened. Yet to scared to know what had happened.

Mom tries to hold in the tear while saying "Daddy passed away. He's in a better place."

Typical. Nobody knew what actually happened. Nor who did it. Polices never tried to investigate it. Wasn't a surprise. Years has passed. Rose has signed up for the police academy. Mostly to investigate the death. Never will she give up.

Big Bully John

Sheniah Everson

On a sunny fall day, there sat Molly Rue James. She was your typical teenager. Good grades, a couple of buns, and boyish ways. On the day before Halloween, she was struck with a bit of karma. Her friends Jason, Max, and Freddy experienced the same punishment.

They had it pretty tough that day in school. Molly's make up went missing, Jason's pants ripped while playing basketball, Max's skateboard was destroyed by his dog, and Freddy was knocked out by the schools BIGGEST bully.

After their long day of torture, then went home to the bad news... the death of each of their moms. They were very much heart broken and torn inside.

Without sleeping or eating they rest of the day, they came up with a plan. They were going to PURGE. They figured nobody could notice them as murders. They took advantage of this halloween night. Especially With all the karma and bad news, they were DONE with what life had to offer.

On the night of halloween, they started with their neighbor, Mr. Wilson, who was asleep. He awoke when he heard the glass break at the front door. Without a chance to fight back, his head was cut off. Blood was splattered across the floors and atop the ceiling. EVERYWHERE.

As they dogged through the refrigerator for a snack they decided who the next victim would be. They kept going down the line from Officer Johnson, to Mr. Nates dog, and so on until they got to BIG BULLY JOHN.

They were doing pretty much everyone a favor by killing Big Bully John. He was the school bully. They didn't feel bad at all.

When the killing spree was over, they linked up at Molly's house for a drink they snuck out of Dr. Mason's fridge.

This long night made them sleepy and hungry. They most definitely felt good, and mostly forgot about their parents death. They made it an annual "thing," to purge on Halloween. Nobody ever heard of the missing and deceased neighbors again. And nobody was SAFE either.

The next Halloween was the purge of children and their dollies.

May the odds be ever in your children's favor.

5 Microfiction

We're Here

E.J. Hilden

This should be easy, he thought. I mean, dang it, I've been sitting here for hours.

He took a feverish look at his phone.

The sound of dripping water.

Echoes.

The smell of mold and mildew, of earth, of rain.

The sound of wind in the trees, and shadows of stones long in the light cast by the caretaker's house.

Something tapped his shoulder.

"We're here," they whispered.

Buzzing

Andrew Brown

The annoying buzzing of the backup generator that has been running ever since the incident suddenly stopped.

The lights all went out with a strange flash of blue.

The man who sought refuge in the abandoned hospital cowered in a corner. Something has entered the building.

And it wasn't human.

Teenage Angie

Sheniah Everson

Teenage Angie didn't know what was next. She was afraid. Family gone. She just hit puberty. Disgusting. Yuck.

There lacked female support, too. So she taught herself to deal with this type of thing.

She went to the guidance counselor for some help.

"Can you Help me?"

"Yes", she replied.

No One To Talk To

Jaelyn Gadsden

Is it true that family leaves?

With a young mind and vivid vocabulary...

What am I to do? No help when needed, and no one to talk to.

But then, as you made your mind up, there is a touch on your shoulder.

"I'm here for you," mom said.

I Wanted To Live

Karisma Hamilton

"Please, no more."

She neglected my endless pleas. She forced it into my mouth and I nearly choked.

"The doctors said you needed more. You can't live like this with your cancer." She forced another spoonful of peas into my mouth.

I hated every moment but I wanted to live.

He Dropped Something

Taniah German

I stumbled off the plane.

This promotion is huge! I needed to settle with the IRS.

"Watch out!"

He dropped something. A suitcase stuffed with cash and a note.

I glanced. I need this money.

Who was he?

I nod, accepting the offer.

I casually disappear into the crowd.

Lost

Lupe Chavez

Alice was lost. She didn't know how to get home.

"HELP!" she yelled.

But no one heard. Then all of the sudden she heard a strange sounds in the brushes.

"I found you," said the stranger.

Alice had nowhere to run. Her friends were gone.

She was lost.

More Heads

Ayleen Galvan

Katalina Trife effortlessly took out the two katanas from their sheaths. She needed heads for her collection.

They were amateurs at best, and tried to threaten her with silly guns. In one skilled slice in the air, Katalina stopped them in their tracks.

And with two taps of her blades together, their hearts were struck, and fell with a thud.

Katalina ran off again, ready to take on more challengers.

6 Holocaust

A Nazi Soldier's Inner Monologue

Kory Singleton

As I stroll through Auschwitz
Head High with PRIDE
I look over and see Jews
Tears in their eyes
To think they expected a good surprise
But I still feel bad
To cause demise
Adolfo told us this thing would
All work out
But up until the invasion
He wouldn't tell,
Tell us what it's about
He asked us to listen and comply we did,
But we can't do this, guys

Look around,
See all the pain on the ground,
There's dead bodies
We treat'em like dogs in the pound.
But…One man can't rebel.
I'll surely be treated
Just like them.
Thrown in a cell
And be starved to death.
I don't really want to die tonight.
I have to go home to my kids and wife.

But wait…
Could it be the exact same for them?
They're bigger men
then we are.
They don't fight
For themselves.
I don't want to cause apocalypse
Because of this dictatorship.
Where are the U. S. BATTLESHIPS?
We can't let this happen again.
We can't forget the cars that
This has brung,
Or else, when we do,
You'll hear the war bells rung.

Now this is just a prediction,
But there may be nuclear weapons
And country to country alliances,
But Germany can't afford to lose.
We don't have the force to win,
Flee to China,
And hope they
Are struck by Cupid,
Or else go through the open door policy.
Oh, can it be
That my mind has changed on me!
That I fought for Adolf
But I know that we are weak.
It's unbelievable
That this is a REALITY.

Torn Away

Jalynn Henryhand

Cold shackles
Walking on cold bare feet
Never stop;
you might get shot
Looking back for hope
Only to be forced in the ghetto

That poor little girl
freezing air
just a blanket between *Life* and *Death*

That silver gate
Sealed all our fates
A single gunshot could be heard
BAM
Soon to be corpse on the dirty streets

It's beautiful wings
Wrapped up in
the foul stench
Burning hearts just in the camp's miles
Gone.

Some might survive
How long til clueless bodies walk
into the gas chambers;
Torches have been lit
Souls on fire

family
Gone.
hope
Gone.
lives
Gone.

Don't forget,
Abuse is beyond recognition
So innocent they were
Blamed for reasons to float in the ears
Listening
Hear the cries
See for your very own eyes
Millions torn.

Wings of Joy

Kiara Brown

Have you felt different about history? I feel that way when I look back at the world. There are marvelous things in the world and there are heartbreaking things. One of them is the Holocaust. When Hitler and the Nazis started massive killing Jewish people, Jewish people's lives were on the line just for believing in their religion. My point of view is that this is a type of discrimination. As Jews run from death, they suffered from hunger, hid in areas and lost love ones.

Not to lie, but there are good things that happened during the Holocaust. We would never had found a Jewish girl's diary. If the Holocaust never happened, we would not know the hatred of the Jewish people, never had books about the culture, and it wouldn't be part of history. This doesn't mean that I want to celebrate the Holocaust. The event is both good and bad.

The Holocaust is like a butterfly to me. It is in a cocoon of darkness but when it is time the butterfly will spread its wings of joy. Don't always look on the bad side of things; look a little deeper and you will see the light. For the people who died during the dark time in the Holocaust, may you fly up like a butterfly to his kingdom and get ready for a new world.

Unreal Fantasy

Hannah Garcia

Skinny bodies,
Pale faces
Living in crowded places
Beaten black and blue
They were blinded like a fool
Lying on their beds,
They think
I can't sleep without a wink

Eyes full of desperation
Dying of starvation
Feeling the dehydration
I swear they hated their nation
Tear stained cheeks,
Chapped lips
Having little bony hips
Living a true nightmare
Is like existing in a fantasy book

Our Pain, Our Sadness

Erica Stoker

Our bodies are no longer temples,
we are shacks made of
thin wood not enough to hold our weight
though it's barely there.

Our smiles never show anymore
but we still try and show our faces
to let the men know
how much of us has withered away.

The bones that are meant to live
inside the skin and hold us up
so we can live are now chiseling
to the surface;

We have never spoken a word to these men
but our religion has spoken volumes.
They hold guns to our heads;
"Don't move" so we don't.

We, the oppressed, the pain, we feel
and try to let the men know
that they are not winning
and they are not going to win.

We still try and hold shallow glimpses
of hope, that we barely have anymore
to our chest but it hits the peeking
rib cage, it leaves a bruise.

It has left many bruises trying
to find hope inside
of something
so very hopeless.

So we don't.

We give up and close our eyes
we trace the silhouettes of our muscles
and our bones and we try to just
breathe…

We breathe and try to believe
that one day the sun will shine
so perfectly on this land
and the men had a good breakfast.

We try and hope to believe that
the men will come
toss our weightless bodies over their shoulder
and take us away.

Was It Worth It?

Ja'Quan Frasier

The gas,
the chemicals,
the lost souls
that were never found.

Sounds of pain and agony
bodies burned into the ground.

Was it worth it?
That cold winter day
with tears, blood and feelings
locked away.
The crying babies
that didn't get to stay.
It was wrong.

Mothers,
fathers,
grandfathers
and sons.
Murdered.

Was it worth it?

The sons and daughters
that never got to say goodbye.
Was it worth it?

While my mother cries
as my dad is shot
right before our eyes
I think to myself
Was it worth it?

The bloodshot veins
running through my sister's eyes.
I think to myself
Was it worth it?

Freedom

Taliyah Bennett

Freedom is what we Jews, Communists, and Unionists
need
As we work and lay in such a heartless place
We need to believe that freedom will come one day
Freedom, Freedom, O Freedom we scream

Freedom is just a taste away
Freedom is just a breath away
O freedom is just a block away
Freedom, Freedom, O Freedom we scream

O when we are freed, I will smell the fresh air
When we are freed, I will be happy for life
When we are freed, I will tell people about my life
Freedom, Freedom, O Freedom we scream

O but freedom is not far
I am ready to explore the sunlight
Jews, Communists, Unionists, we will be freed
Freedom, Freedom, O Freedom we wait

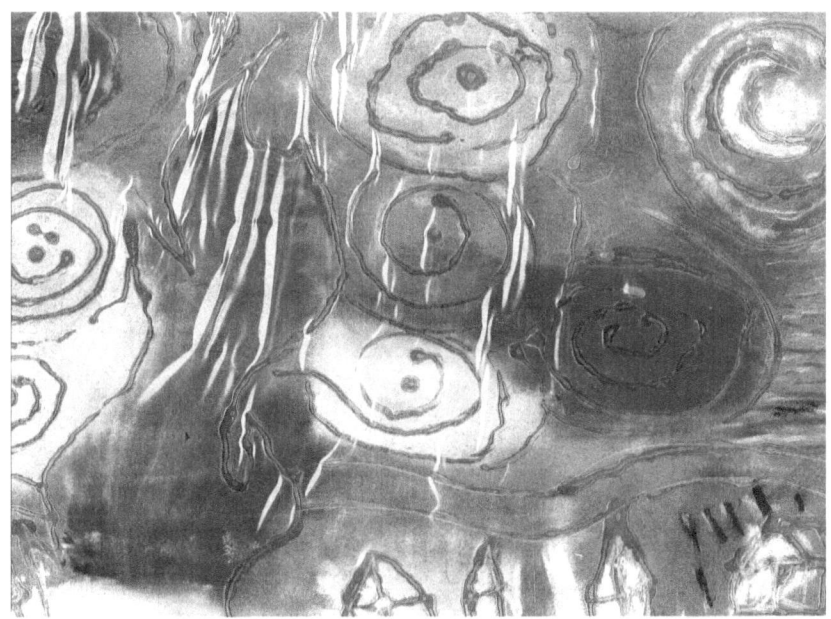

World Fading to Black

Morgan McClure

The truck jolted as we drove across the bumpy road. The snow impaired our sight causing us to continuously have to read adjust our course.

Up ahead a shape came into view. As we drove closer, the shape defined. The truck jolted to a stop. I opened the door, letting the cold winds fill up the space of the truck.

My feet sunk the moment they hit the snow, causing

me to exert more effort in each step. Soon, in front of me stood the gate of Buchenwald, on it inscribed the phrase "Jedem das seine." To each his own, and today this shall become my home.

Guards patrolled the top of the gate house. I walked towards the doors, then opened the iron gates; this led to a wide open courtyard. Snow was lightly covering the ground compared to outside. A soldier walked up and saluted me, and I, of course, returned the honor.

He said that he was here to show me around. As I walked around the grounds, I constantly eyed the Jews. They were in the most horrible of conditions, where they were missing limbs, or they were almost starved to death; and around them always stood dogs that barked and soldiers that glared.

I did a quick prayer to God, to help these men, or at least let me help them as their new Obersoldat, a senior soldier.

Then we stopped in front of a long brick building with barbed wire on each side. In between the building and the wire fence, there was a courtyard which was occupied by dogs and soldiers. I walked inside the building and the prisoners instantly stood, or at least those who could still stand. After my introduction by the soldier who showed me around, I quickly walked back out of the building, not being able to stand the state that the prisoners were in. Then I retired for the night at the barracks.

I woke to the sound of the alarm ringing beside my bed. I quickly got up and did my morning routine. Teeth brushed, hair combed, suit applied, wrinkles smoothed, tea drank.

After I finished, I set out for the prisoners' barracks. I ushered them out towards the Gustloff Factory, where they would be working from now on. I oversaw them as they worked, making the rifles that would fortify the German army.

As I was watching, one of the Obergefreiter guards motioned towards an older prisoner that was falling behind. He told me to beat him, to show him that I was in command, and that I did not tolerate slow workers. I was told these are the standards...that I was to beat into their heads. I looked at the old man and hesitated. How could I beat him? How could I bring myself to do it?

Then, before I could stop it, one of the guards beat him in my stead. They beat him while he screamed. The whole factory had grown quiet, watching. That's all I could do...watch... watch as he beat him to a bloody pulp. I began to hate myself for doing nothing, but what could I have done? Shown I was a traitor?

No, I could not, so I just prayed for God to forgive me. When I got home that day I raged. I flipped my desk, threw my lamps, and when it was over, I quietly slumped down against the door, crying, cradling myself.

Today I woke with renewed vigor. It had been a few days since the beating. After that, the workers had kept up quota, so no one else was beaten. I then set out for the prisoners' barracks to rally up the prisoners and herd them over to the Gustloff factory.

After working for hours, which seemed to stretch out forever, the prisoners were called back for lunch. But, as they waited in the courtyard, they were forced away from the food table. I, confused as well, asked another soldier what was going on. Apparently a warden had been hung for conspiring against the camp with the prisoners. The prisoners who had helped him were getting hung as an example to the others.

I watched intently as the prisoners walked up to the platform and prepared to be hung. They solemnly stood there, accepting their fate. One at a time, they were hung. Some cursed and spat upon Germany's name; some were just silent.

It came to the last prisoner. It was a little boy, no older than 12. His sad face pleaded while the noose was hung around his neck, and asked where is God, whether Christian, Muslim, or any God could stop this, or to give him the strength to stop this.

I prayed and pleaded but I stood unmoving, petrified. I saw as his body fall, noose tightly wrapped around his neck, and as he fell, I felt that noose. As he choked his life away, I felt mine fading. I could not believe that God could let this happen, so in that moment I stopped believing in any God. I was horrified that I could not have stopped it, therefore, in that moment, I stopped believing in myself. As he hung, I felt the colors of the world fade to black and grey, in that moment I stopped believing in a world of order and good.

In that moment, I died, and a new me was born. One who whipped as hard as he could, one who killed any who got in his way, and lastly one who didn't believe anything could be good, honest, or righteous. One who believed in Man's Inhumanity to Man.

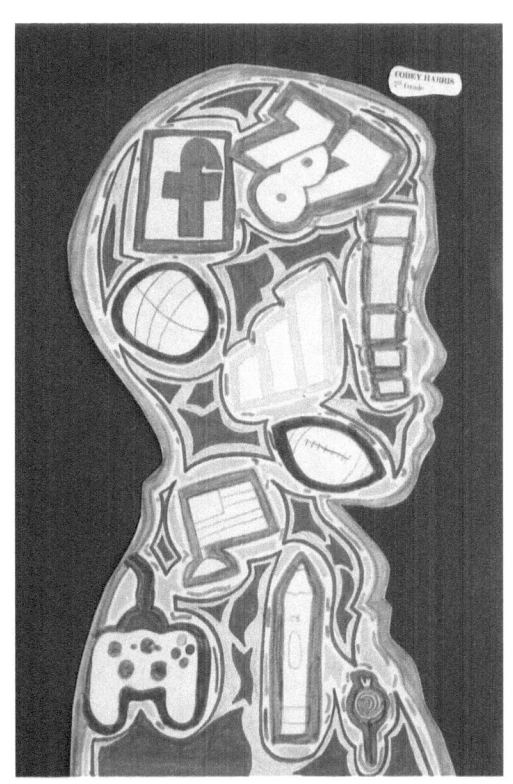

7 On Spring

I Love Spring

Caitlin McCants

Spring is here!
Which means all the pollen and bees and other insects
I hate come out.
When Spring comes its so pretty sometimes.
The sky is a pretty blue with the white clouds
and the bright sun that's showing.
To me Spring is beautiful.
Spring kind of reminds me of summer.
It's warm and all the Spring and Summer clothes come out.
I love Spring.

Spring is here

Kiara Milligan

Spring is here.
You know what that means...
Spring break is what I cheer.
But wasps and bees...
The only thing I fear.
But I love that
Spring is here!!

Yass boo I want spring break too begin.

Spring is a thing

Jemar Jones

Spring is a cool thing
Everyday is a sunny day
It's always a great day to play
Spring is a cool thing

Why Do I Keep Sneezing?

Kayla R. Cannady

Why do I keep sneezing?
Three times in a row.
Has Spring arrived?
Did we get rid of the snow?

My eyes itch
While my nose swells.
My face is puffed up.
Spring hasn't started very well.

The little kids play,
While I'm inside stuck with tissue.
Claritin-D pills everywhere.
Do you not see the issue?
I don't care for the flowers.
They don't mean much at all.
I just want to end the allergies.
Why can't it be Fall?

Spring is finally here

Zaviera Brown

Spring is finally here
Seeing the tree's in the breeze
Hearing the bees sting
Spring is finally here

For better, and for worse

Mackenzie Cook

Changing of the seasons.
Fresh start Change.
New people
Saying good bye whether it's temporary
Or forever.
Falling leaves.
Growing flowers.
Sunshine and happiness.
Cold, depressing winters.
Everything changes
For better
And for worse.

It was Spring

Karisma Hamilton

When I woke up to check mailbox, I saw weeds.
The tall, ugly ones that deserved to be cut immediately.
"If weeds were here…"
My thought was interrupted by a certain sneeze.
A sneeze that only made a "Kachoo" sound when there was
sticky, yellow stuff all over the place.
I realized it was Spring.

Except for Martin

Kamron Washington

Spring was there.
Everyone lit-up with joy and ran outside in a hurry.
They looked around outside at the beautiful flowers that were
freshly pollinated.
They saw butterflies, bees, etc.
Everyone was so surprised except for Martin.
He had really bad allergies and couldn't go outside.
So everyone went in to hang out with him.

It's a Love or Hate Thing

Lucy Diaz

Spring, its a love and hate thing.
No more gloom all you see is flowers bloom.
The town filled with color, there is no more wonder.

Kids playing outside, but my allergies to pollen
makes me stay inside.
Hearing the birds sing , but the bees are starting to sting.
When you go outside all you see is people running
around…
Like please sit down
Getting some sun, having fun.

But Spring makes me realize that there is yet
another season to come
Which means another year is going to end,
and school has to start again.

After the Volcano

Zinnia Beard

Once upon a time, there lived a village of fairies. They couldn't fly because the winter snow froze their wings until Spring.

Each day, Lizzy the water fairy would go to Lary the unicorn, and ask him how many days would the snow stay on the ground. Lizzy loved the flowers, and being able to fly during the Spring.

He wanted winter to end quickly, so she took a trip to Smurfopolis, and asked Papa Smurf to make a great wind, that would last for two days, and after the great wind it would become Spring.

Papa Smurf didn't like messing up the seasons, but he dearly missed Spring too, so he gave Lizzy a special seed, and told her to plant the seed at midnight, or the special seeds powers would go away. Lizzy did as she was told, and left Smurfopolis, with a big smile on her face.

When Lizzy ran home she tripped and dropped the seed down a volcano. She felt so bad she went back to Papa Smurf as a heavy wind picked up.

All of a sudden, volcano juice came up from the volcano and blew a mighty wind. The volcano juice was so hot it burned everyone to small tiny specks.

After the volcano, it became Spring. No one was able to see it.

The Flower

Zinnia Beard

The flower that grows where nobody knows.
In the dark it sits waiting to get picked.
Though confidence shows and nobody knows.
In the dark it sits waiting to get picked.

The sun shined, and touches its pedals.
It springs to life in the beautiful meadow.
The snow dries up and the kids all play.
It once was winter and now its Spring.

That was the flower
When the seasons changed.

Spring Break

Sheniah Everson

I'm ready For Spring break.
I'm tired of
Homework,
Teachers,
Students,
Bell Ringers,
Walking in lines,
Waking up at seven.
I'm tired of
Every single thing.

A moment to re-evaluate life

Sheniah Everson

It's almost the end of the year.

Everyone is leaving.

Not everyone...

Just Hope it's you.

This is last close to...

Being the last quarter.

Everyone's grades need to be up

So we can all hold up that cup.

8th grade ceremony just around the corner.

If you slack now,

You won't be getting a diploma.

Let's all take

A Moment

To

Reevaluate

Life

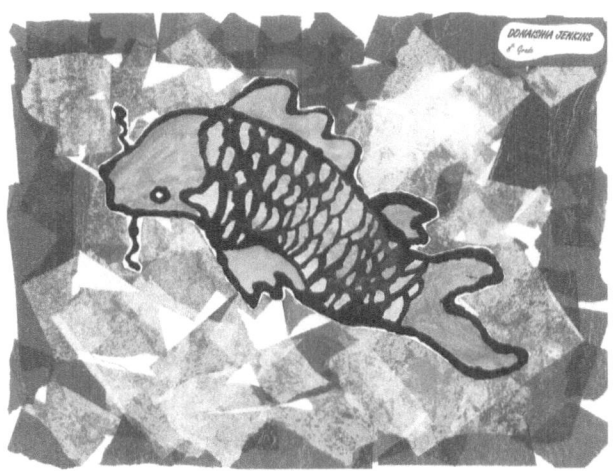

Bury the Hatchet

Seth Rivers

The air begins to turn warm,which we consume.
The brown grass begins to sprout flowers,they begin to
bloom.
No more long pants, mine are short
Now that its warmer I can play on the court.
An extra hour of sleep helps me realize, that there will be
no more leaves falling from the sky.
I can go in the pool now,
Now I don't have a frown.
I leave behind my past
Wow, how time moves so fast
I just had on 4 jackets
Now I am ready to go to the beach, and sit on a blanket
The Fall is gone so just forget it.
Prepare for the Spring and bury the hatchet.

BLAKE HANLEY

It went in little ways

Omigi Grant

In the Spring of the year, in the Spring of the year,
I walked the road beside my dear.
The trees were black where the bark was wet.
I see them yet, in the Spring of the year.

He broke me a bough of the blossoming peach
That was out of the way and hard to reach.
In the Fall of the year, in the Fall of the year,
I walked the road beside my dear.

The rooks went up with a raucous trill.
I hear them still, in the Fall of the year.
He laughed at all I dared to praise,
And broke my heart in little ways.

Year be Springing or year be Falling,
The bark will drip and the birds be calling.
There's much that's fine to see and hear
In the Spring of a year, in the Fall of a year.

'Tis not love's going hurt my days.
But that it went in little ways.

As soon as Spring arrives...

Ayleen Galvan

As soon as Spring arrives,
We start preparing for Summer.
Disregard the flowers.
What does summer mean to me?

A new fashion season!
But Summer always brings the coolest things to store.
Like..
Shorts to stay cool...
Short Shorts to look cool...
Booty Shorts to look dumb...
Cute skirts that brush the knees...
Sexy skirts that brush your thighs...
Crop tops to look sweet and sassy and even cropier crop
tops to look like a try hard...
Sheer tights for the modest...
Mock thigh highs for the cuties...
Real thigh highs for the fierce...
Flower headbands for the hippie...
Pastel shirts for the hipster...
Expensive tees for the hot topic goth...
And new earrings for the tweens...
Flip Flops that pop...
Flip Flops that stay...
Flip Flops that melt into the sidewalk...
Sneakers for the summer joggers...
Vans for the summer casual...

And sandals for the pure divas...
And Swimsuit are everywhere now.
Bikinis for the open books...
Tankinis for those with something to hide...
One pieces for the little one...
Swim-skirts for the shy...
Speedos for the fun guys...
And little beach hats to match your sunglasses.

But still, maybe in the way back,
You'll find a skinny jean or two.
Maybe there's one last slit sweater.
There could be a beanie.
Or maybe a good scarf.
But you won't be sad, because come August...
Winter clothes are back!

Snowflake

Andrew Brown

It was winter, but now it's Spring.
They say it won't snow again 'till next Winter,
but one day, I swear, I felt a snowflake fall on my head.
Yet, for some reason, nobody believes me
to this day.

I Hate Spring

Solomon Adams

There is way too much love in Spring time
So I'll sprinkle in some hate.
Too many kids are screaming and frolicking,
Preparing for Spring ſreak.

If I could stop Spring from coming,
I would with so much ease.
I despise the smell of burnt grills,
and the stings of honeybees.

Why must the bright sunshine
Be so blinding?
And why is the rain so constant,
As if it were rewinding?

I hate the annoying mosquitoes
Stinging me constantly.
I hate the golden pollen,
Bringing back my allergies.

I'd much rather have Christmas
And let the sleigh bells ring.
But these are just a few reasons
as to why I hate Spring.

The Season

Tilayah Bennett

The season is gone
The colors have changed.
Sunshine and clouds
Are all that remain.

And cold Winter nights
Will never be the same.
Because The trees have
Shed their last leaf.

All the winds in the world
Blowing at high speeds.
Carrying dead leaves
From far away.

Leaving the poor trees
Naked and afraid.
With new clothes coming,
And the sounds of birds singing.

All the animals in the world
Will finally awake.
Because Spring is here,
They don't want to be late.

Why, Spring?

Taniah German

Lord knows that Spring just ain't my thing
I hate that it makes my nose sting
Pollen gets to me
My eyes be itchy
That season just makes my head ring

There is something different

Josh Huckabee

As the seasons change,
So does the day.

Summer the days are longer,
And Winter the days is shorter.

Fall the leaves change color and fall.
Winter the grass and trees die.

Spring leaves come back and
Plants trees and grass come back to life.

Winter it is cold.
Summer it is hot.

In every season
there is something different.

Everyone Goes Crazy

Tremell Bowens

As the season changes,
Flowers come and go.
The grass color changes,
Kids are ready for Spring Break.

They may even be ready
To end the year.

I know I am.

Going to the beach,
Meeting pretty girls at the mall,
Going out to parties,
Basically anything you want.

It's not like you have school
To worry about anymore…

it's almost summer.

When they know that
It's only like 2 more months
Of school left,
Everyone goes crazy.

8 Camping Stories

The Trip Was Fun

Shydazja Wright

The trip was fun
Even though there wasn't a lot of sun
It was fun to get away and start this wonderful spring break
Animals coming out at night
Scaring everyone who came in sight
Late nights early mornings
the trip was fun

Never Sleeping

Jasmine Sanders

never sleeping
never sleeping again
raccoon here
raccoon there

was I seeing things
or believing I'm just dreaming
kick start here
kick start on Kayla

food was on fleet
drink on the other hand
wasn't that sweet
it was alright

glad its the last year

Not Anything like The Hood

Sheniah Everson

Long nights
Scary noises
No ones in sight
No little kid toys

We ate very nasty food
Couldn't get in the groove
We didn't sleep well
The boys always smelled

Canoeing, paint balling, pool was cold
Couldn't go sleep
Ghost in our souls
Creepy

Girls brought drama
Should've stayed with their mama
Overall it good
Not anything like the hood

HARLEY LEWIS
8th Grade

The Last Trip

Sheniah Everson

Today was an exciting day for Angelic. This was the day she was waiting for for months.

"Are you ready", her grandmother asked.

She responded in a very energetic voice, "Yes gran-nyma, be right there."

While on an empty stomach, she was eager to sit down and eat what her grandmother had fixed for her.

"Good Morning, honey" G-ma exclaimed cheerfully. She informed Angelic to eat up quick so they can head out for the camping trip. As Angelic ate her nutritious breakfast, she thought about all if the things she's was going to get into today. Although she was iffy about going, she as was excited to see what the day had in store for her.

"Okay all done grandma", she said while walking out the door.

Pulling up to Jerry Zucker Middle school, Angelic started to get butterflies. This was her last year going on this trip and she wanted it to be the best. She wanted to make her mark on that campground.

"Thank you granny ma, I'm going to have a great time," she said aloud, while struggling with her bags.

Grannyma responded with a weird look on her face, "You're only going one night. You really need all of those bags?"

Angelic giggled and closed the door. While walking to class she got the sly comments of, "Wow, that's a lot of stuff." Or "You're only going one night", or "You packed your whole house right." Angelic didn't care though, because she always packed like that.

"Good Morning sunshine sugar plum candy apple", her teacher welcomed as she walked in. Because Spring break started once she would get back, Angelic had to collect her work.

"It's time to load the bus", Ms. Mossiri exclaimed. Mossiri was always on top of things, so it was sure enough going to be fun if she came. The bus ride was very quiet going to Camp Ho Na Wah. Angelic felt pretty down. This was their last year and she want to turn up. Angelic played some music and got people to tag along with singing.

After forty-five minutes of riding, they finally approached a sign that said, "Welcome to 'Camp Ho Na Wah' ." Angelic was bursting into tears in the inside.

"Okay everyone eat up, it's important you stay

hydrated, we have a long day ahead of us," Mr. Perlmatter went on. He always talks a lot so that was no surprise. Everyone ate their lunch and got ready to explore the camp and choose cabins.

When they got to the campsite, it was exactly like last year.

"Are you sleeping with me"? Beyoncé asked curiously. She didn't know what cabin they wanted, but they knew they were going to sleep somewhere, and they were going to sleep well.

"Everyone get ready for your first activity," the teachers yelled. Everyone was settling in their cabins getting ready.

"Are you guys ready?" Angelic asked, making new friends. She figured they were cool folks, and they would click.

Everyone was tired of walking and worn out by 5:30. They were ready to eat and shut it down. Once dinner was over, they went to the campfire to gather for s'mores and cookies. At the campfire there were people dancing and singing. Everyone was happy and getting along. Angelic felt renewed. This was what she wanted. "C-A-M-P-F-I-R-E-S-O-N-G song", sponge bob played in the back ground. After Mr. Perlmatter dismissed the boys, the girls got a chance to stay and sing some more.

"My feet hurt," somebody mumbled, while walking back to our campsite. When they were reunited it was now almost 1.

"We should just join cabins, and we'll bring in some cots," Angelic's' new squad suggested. As they got set up for bed, there was no turning down. They stayed up and turned up some more. We got a little tired so, everyone just settled down and started doing some confessions.

Being rudely interrupted by some other campers, Angelic said "Were y'all talking about me, because I thought I heard my name." Angelic was already grouchy so she didn't care how anyone took her attitude that night. Responding rudely, she informed her that nobody talking about her and that she should return to her cabin and go to sleep. All dogs broke loose after that comment. That almost led to some violence. Angelic was furious but guess what. She surely slept good that might.

"Okay everyone it's time to clean our cabins so we could head back," a teacher informed. Angelic wasn't ready to go home. She felt like everything was just getting started.

She really liked camping because she was always ready to get down and dirty. Approaching the school she was upset. She didn't want to go home, but she had to. It was time to get back to business. She was most definitely not ready for the work she had to do when she got back. She already knew Mr. Hilden was about to run and sure enough he did. Angelic was waiting outside for her ride and got a tense feeling of joy. She was happy to know she got the opportunity to go camping, and she would love to do it again, if she could.

News Report thingy
(I guess we'll call it that)

Ayleen Galvan

BREAKING CAMP NEWS

At about 2 am Friday morning, while the principle believed the girls were asleep, one cabin of 8th graders were determined to turn up and gossip all night. 12 diverse ladies crammed together to just have an easy night of sleep over fun, telling who they liked and didn't like, who was broke up and who got back together. Of course, at 2 am, everyone was all getting sleepy and was just settling down. When suddenly, one 8th grade camper from about three cabins away appeared with some questions, the conversation went as such:

"Hey, um I think you guys were talking about me"

"No we weren't, go back"

"Well I just thought you guys were talking about me"

"Well DON'T THINK WHAT YOU DON'T KNOW!"

"Listen here, I came here nice and calm-"

"Well then you can LEAVE nice and calm!!"

This made that girl throw down her flashlight, and as some reported, "ready to fight". But the girls were even more enraged when they saw that this camper wasn't alone. In fact, about 6 or 7 more girls were behind the visitor, pulling her back and shouting at her to "calm down" and "stop". When the girls on the left half the cabin saw the squad, an explosion of shouting and arguing started. When they calmed down, the girls all whipped out their phones and called everyone who was awake to retell what just happened.

The next day, or, next 5 hours, their was noticeable tension between the groups of girls. But both groups wanted to pretend nothing happened. And the small, uninvolved groups admit they are slightly scared about what's going to happen when they come back from Spring Break.

Back to you...

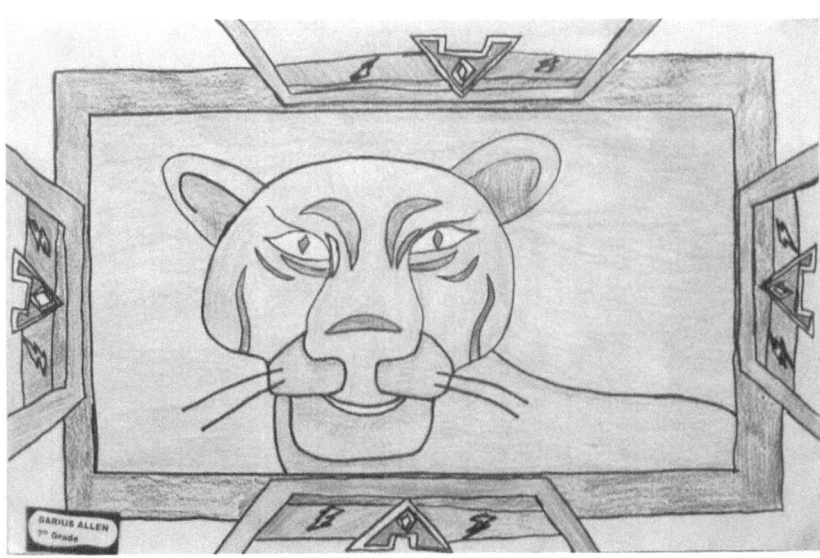

9 On Heroes and Heroism

A Hero To Me

Anauticah Fulton

A hero to me
Is someone who's wise
Some who's brave
Someone who's giving
Someone's caring and lovable
A hero doesn't have to be a person
It can be a dog
It can be a cat
It can be a reptile
It can be a mammal
A hero to me is someone
That I would want to be
Because its a lot of rewards that come with it
Everybody can be a hero no matter what

A Hero Isn't Always Strong

Necey Gillyard

A hero isn't always strong
A hero don't need to fly
A hero helps you with anything
A hero is strong about his/her actions
A hero is sometimes powerful
A hero helps the world
A hero helps you when you are in trouble
A hero can face anything
A hero keeps you out of danger
A hero has abilities to do anything
A hero can be me or you or anyone you believe in
A hero is not no bully or push you around
A hero can be someone who has gone throw so much
And is still standing
A hero stops crime
A hero can stop bullies
A HERO CAN BE ANY ONE YOU ONLY HAVE TO BELIEVE!!

What A Hero Is To ME

Zaviera Brown

What a hero is to me ...

A hero to me is someone good
A hero is someone who helps
A hero is a forgiving person

A hero is brave.
A hero is someone who fights.
A hero is someone who saves lives.
A hero is a strong person.

A hero is someone real.

A hero to me is my mom.
My mom fights everyday.
My mom helps me.
My mom cares for me.
My mom is my unlimited hero.

Heros are brave
Heros are kind
Heros fight
Heros aren't just make believe characters we have.

Heros all around this world.
You may not notice one but there is always a hero right
in front of you.
One day you can be that hero.

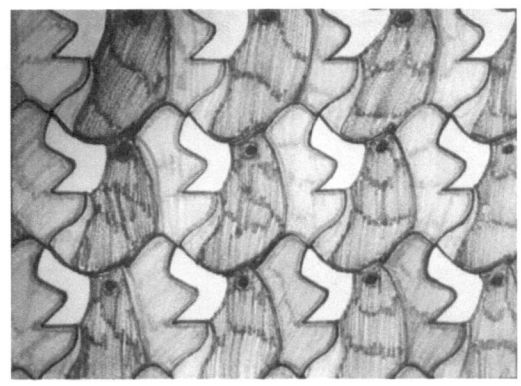

My Point of View

Angie Solis

In my point of view a hero is…

Someone who thinks of others before themselves.
One whom forgives everybody.
The one who is quite kind.
She is an inspirational person.
Shes very thoughtful.
Doesn't care what other people say.
One who will go so far just to help that one person.
Yeah, perhaps she/he doesn't have a costume
Nor a sidekick.
She/he doesn't have powers
But that doesn't make a hero a hero.
What makes them a hero is being smart,
kind,
thoughtful.

And that's what truly counts.

A Hero Doesn't Have To Fly

Caitlin McCants

A hero doesn't always fly
Or have superpowers
Or supervision
Or know how to fly
He or she does have to fight or battle a person to save
the world
They don't have to have a cap
Or a bike that transform into a car
Or any magical thing
This hero could be a normal person
Who doesn't have any superpowers
Or any powers at all
A hero just has to put they mind to what they wanna do
The hero needs to be loved
Have people tell them they can do it
Feel special about themselves
A hero needs to be strong

They Achieve Their Missions

Tilayah Bennett

A hero to me means that you're brave
You are willing to make sacrifices.
You are willing to risk your life for a love one or someone else.
You go out your way and time to protect a love one
or someone else.

A Hero is kind hearted.
He/she makes mistakes but fix their mistakes.
Sometimes they help out of kindness or
sometimes because they want to.

They have talent and skills.
A hero goes through challenges.
They have boundaries.
A hero has faith.
They can relate to real people.
They can't give up.
They can't doubt themselves.
They respect others.

They achieve their missions.

A Hero Doesn't Always Have A Cape

Jackson Chestnut

A hero doesn't always have a cape.
They don't have to fly.
They don't need superpowers.
They don't need unstoppable powers.
All a hero needs is himself.
They have to help others.
They don't even need to be that serious.
They could just take someone to work.
A hero could be anyone.
They are intelligent.
They are caring.
And last but not least brave and daring.
I think a hero should be recognized.
I think a hero should be loved.
I think a hero should be rewarded.
I think they are special.

Are YOU a Hero?

Johnieyer Bragg

To be a hero
you don't have to be able to read minds
or fly like a bird
A hero stands by those who stood by them
A hero doesn't have to stop time
so they can think about
what they're going to do,
they just do it.
Heroes help others
with no hesitation at all
or no expectations of a reward
Heroes don't care if they mess up
because they're human
and they accept it
A hero will try and keep trying
until they do it
even if it kills them
because they know
they're helping innocent people.
Heroes can be young
or old,
a mother
or a father,
a son
or daughter,
a sister
or brother.

You could save a life as a hero
or you could just show some one
that you care
as a hero.
Heroes are different in their own ways
and that's what make them heroes.
You could know if someone's a hero
or they could be unknown.
Heroes protect the innocent
and stop the bad.
Heroes may have enemies
but they have their loved ones
so they're okay
with having a few enemies.
If heroes were to stop trying
or they gave up
things could go bad.
You might not know it
but heroes are everywhere
from your parents
to your teachers.
They may make it look easy
but heroism is hard
and it takes a lot
of work.

Are YOU a hero?

To Me, A Hero is...

Alicia Alexandrea White

"To me my hero is…"
My hero is Powerful.
She is creative.
She is well known for her independence.
She is a nice person.

"To me my hero is…"
My hero is forgiving.
She is a forgiver.
She learns new positive things.
If she makes a promise, she will keep it

"To me my hero is…"
She is awesome in the things she does.
She learns from her mistakes.
She finds a new way.
She makes a new way to do stuff.

"To me my hero is…
She makes a new life for herself.
She knows what to say to someone when you are down.
She helps you when you need someone.
She will back you up when you need someone to lean on.

"To me my hero is..."
She is someone who doesn't do bad.
She is someone who finds a conflict
and makes a resolution.
If she makes a crime she will do the time.
She learns from her mistakes.

"To me my hero is..."
She is a great leader.
She helps other people become a leader.
She is a great person inside and out.
She is a person who stands up for what she believes in.

"To me my hero is all of the above"

A Hero is Courageous

Josh Huckabee

A hero is courageous
A hero is brave
A hero stands up for himself
A hero is just himself
A hero does not try to act like someone else
A hero tries to do the right thing
A hero tries to stay out of trouble
A hero does not always know that he is a hero
He could just be himself and be a hero
He could help someone else and be a hero
He could do the right thing to be hero
A hero could face challenges
Such as getting made fun of
Not getting respect
Having trouble staying out of trouble
Or could even get respect everyday as his challenge

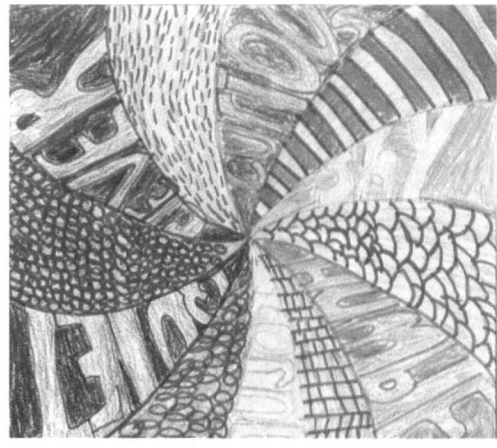

A Couple of Heroes

Josh Huckabee

Frederick Douglass had excellent heroism. He had incredible heroism because, the first thing is he stood up for his rights. He stood up for his rights by escaping slavery.

He escaped slavery because the first thing is; he did not have his rights. The second thing is the slave owners did not treat them fairly. They called the slaves the names that they did not want to be called or unpleasant names. The third reason why he is a perfect example of what heroism is he was a good role model: to kids today, and also to slaves back then. The fourth reason is that he taught himself to read and write. Learning that most likely helped him with his ongoing stressful but successful life.

Abraham Lincoln is a excellent example of heroism as well. First he wanted to end slavery. The second reason is lthat he ed us to our (United States of America) freedom. He tried to lead us to our freedom by bringing the Union and the Confederate States of America back together to form one country again. The third reason is that he was the 16th president of the U.S.A. The fourth reason he shows heroism is he led the Union side of the Civil War.

I think that Frederick Douglass and Abraham Lincoln are both terrific examples of heroism. I told why they are above. They were both big hearted men, and also perfect examples of heroism.

10 On Going to High School

Coming of age is true

Patrick Myers

Believe it or not you gotta do what you gotta do
Grades are important and times is flying
You're working hard while your teacher is yelling "no whining"
It's time to mature and look at life
Not time to play around and ride bikes
It's time to apply for classes
It's almost time
Coming of age is true
It just takes time

Am I ready?

Kamron Washington

I wonder what they are going to talk about. Thoughts travel around in my head, fears of what is going to happen. Am I ready for high school? What if I'm not? I will only have to figure out on my own. I walk over slowly, worried of what is to come.

I turn back and let someone take my place and continue on my work. I thought to myself why is this significant I know I'm not going to that school. What is the point any way?

My time decreased. I didn't know what to do. I talk to myself. I can do this. I'm ready for high school, I work hard and I have achieved a lot, it'll be simple. I walk slowly with a little less fear. I was ready I sat down and listened to what the lady had to say. The words really inspired me to work hard and do very well. I thought a new school, making new friends, seeing different people. I thought I am going to miss this school. I thought about all the good moments at this school.

I have to go to a different school but who will I be? I still have to find myself at this new school but I'm willing to do that as long as I get my education.

A new school with new faces.

I will be all alone.

No friends nobody.

All alone.

Once again I'm that shy kid who won't talk.

Will the bullying begin again?

I will just have to see.

Hopefully it won't but when I get there I will see.

The work will increase but I can handle this.

It won't get too difficult if I work hard.

No interruptions and no distractions.

I can do this if I work hard and try.

New Everythings

Sheniah Everson

I'm very speechless
Summery day
new faces
New everything
I'm very speechless
School supplies
Looking every which way
New everything
I'm lost
I'm confused
I'm speechless
New everything
I'm shy
I'm particular
I'm the new kid
New everything
New faces
New clothes
New shoes
New Everything
I finally made it
I'm here to stay
I'm here to make a mark
New everything
Burke High, are you ready?
Am I ready?
Because this is the time
New everythings.

And That is That

Saleema El-Amin

Today I registered for Stall.

It was very fun and full of amusement. I guess I say this because I have been dreaming about this for a while now.

Since I was little, I always set high standards for myself and set goals for me to do big things. Sitting down in that chair and registering did a lot of things, and had me thinking a lot of questions.

Am I really ready?

How am I going to adapt?

How am I going to bring my grades up to get my credits?

I already have 1 and a half credits from Haut Gap. It was really a reality check. I'm growing up, new hair, clothes, shoes, uniform, boyfriend.

But school comes first. I have chosen multiple classes that will benefit my future.

When I grow up, I want to be an interpreter and translator of foreign languages. Particularly Arabic, because I know a lot of it (I'm Muslim).

This experience has definitely inspired me to pull my grades up a little more and try harder. Not everyone gets into honors, and I'm kinda blowing off my opportunity. I have support and backup. I am also looking forward to Latin, and band. And that is that.

I'll Get Over It

Briashmel Bell

Signing up for high school today was really fun but it was more of a reality check. I got to see all the paperwork of my classes and the options for extracurricular activities. Although I'm not going to Stall, it was still fun because I know that my high school will be similar.

It's a little scary knowing that we only have three months left in middle school.

It's bittersweet because I'm excited for high school but I'm a little sad leaving my friends in middle school.

It's exciting being this close to going to high school. I plan to be the best I can in the ninth grade. I'm going to strive for all A's and Miss Freshman. I think high school will be fine and I might be nervous at first but I'm sure I'll get over it.

When I Grow Up

Karisma Hamilton

To me filling out that high school paper was like signing a paper that gave away my childhood. I know that after this, I'll no longer be a little girl.

This makes me sad.

No more worrying about when my favorite ortie cartoon is coming on and no more crying over my dolls being broken.

Now I have to face the real world. I know about these 4 years, I'll be an adult.

Now I'll have to worry about when the bills are going to be paid and crying over being fired.

This just made me realize that I'm maturing and I'll have to grow up some day.

So, this was disappointing to me.

But at least I know when I grow up, I've graduated and I'll have an opportunity to grow up and be happy.

How Fast Time Flies

Omigi Grant

Registering for Stall made me realize how fast time flies. I'm growing up. But my experience was cool, I got to sign up for the classes that I wanted. I also know that my schedule will be how I want it. Registering was just fun, because it felt real before, but now it feels even more real. I think I will enjoy Stall.

School Comes First

Anauticah Fulton

My experience registering for Stall was very interesting because I got to pick some of my classes and also find out what classes I have to take. Honestly I'm satisfied with my classes. All of them are just what I wanted. Going to high school is just one more step closer to me going to college and becoming a successful young lady. If I do what I'm suppose to do in high school and not make the wrong decision I believe I can make it

I'm going to leave a lot of close friends

Jemar Jones

Registering for high school was pretty cool. I got to see what type of classes they had and I got to pick which ones I wanted.

Thinking about high school makes me feel good. It makes me feel like I'm growing up and that I'm free. I can walk the halls and I don't have to have a teacher staring down my back.

Sometimes I don't like thinking about high school because when I graduate the eighth grade and go to high school I'm going to be leaving a lot of my close friends.

My transition to High School

Matthew Greene

Going to high school will not be a big deal for me. I cannot wait till I go. The transition will be sad but high school is just another step to freedom. I mean the government forces me to go to school (I never chose to). But I will go to college because I love money. So basically I am just going to learn, to work, to get money.

Most people say high school is bad but I love high school. I mean I love the way I am seeing it. I have seen lots of junior high and high school movies that say it is a terrible experience but I don't think so. It's all about perspective. And they have not really told the good sides in movies. And here I am to tell you the good things about it. You get to make new friends. Really some people just want to go to high school to escape drama. And they just need new people to hang out. Another reason is you can learn. Learn some new things from Extra curriculums you would like. I just love art so bad. I mean who doesn't love Disney? Another thing is you get to experience deep stuff you notice on TV.

High School is going to be the bomb. I am really just sugar high right now. People who just don't want to grow up, I mean, grow up! (It's not all that bad). Can y'all not? And those who agree with me, "Whoop, whoop!"

High school is gonna be way too extravagant! I guess going to high school will be a big deal for me in a way.

A Quote about High School

Solomon Adams

My life is speeding up way too fast. It's like I was just playing in the sandbox last week and now I'm about to put on a cap and gown.

No more kiddy stuff anymore. This is taking on step into the real world. Time to be responsible, respectful, and hardworking. No more goofing around in class because what I do now will effect me for the rest of my life. I am finally about to be released from the cages of childhood so I can soar through the reality of adulthood.

Finally I will truly reap the success of my hard work and accomplishments.

People will now take me seriously. My eyes are truly opened , and I am ready to go.

It's already too late

Ebonie Mustipher

The whole process with enrolling was kind of hard. It was hard to choose the classes I wanted to be in. There were a lot of choices and I didn't want to end up in a class I don't like. That was the only thing that was hard about it though.

Honestly it is very nerve racking to be this close to high school. Like now is the time where we need to be extra serious. Because if y'all play around its going to show up on your permanent records. Then later on when you apply for college then you're most likely going to end up in a very crappy college. Like we need to stop and be mature because pretty much your whole life depends on how you do in high school.

Like, say if you want to be a doctor. So you're playing around in class and not turning in your work. Then you continue to do the same until like your last year then BOOM!

Its already too late unless your going to start high school over again. You're not going to be a doctor like you wanted. You may end up working at McDonalds getting like no money what so ever. But I'm very serious y'all need to get your act together and be serious before its too late. Unless that is your dream to work at McDonalds.

Which I seriously hope it's not.

You're kidding, right?

Jaelyn Gadsen

What is life?
Is it people graduating?
Making it somewhere in life?
Or is it going to jail?
Making a reputation as a bad person...

Why is it that
Kids want to kill each other
To make a point
Only to end up
In jail or 6 feet under?

Why can't they just go to school?
Learn how to make better choices?
Go somewhere in life?
Show the world there's more to life?

Why is it hard to write a paper,
But so easy to pull a trigger?

Just think about
What we could have done.

I Thought I was Crazy

Saleema El-Amin

I came to Zucker from almost one hour away,
I sounded so "geechie" everybody thought I was cray.

I'm not gon' lie, I'm an island girl. Comin' to Zucker
just changed my world.

My old school was very jack and was loaded with
swag. Although we had a lot of drugs, and the kids sometimes acted so bad! Us being rebellious, they punished
the whole school.

So we didn't go on many field trips and, in our minds,
that was cruel.

My experience at Zucker, at first, wasn't ever so great.

When I made my arrival, I had a lot on my plate. It
took a while to adapt. I moved up further on the map.

This school is highly involved...

So my pre-paradigms about this school were solved.

I met my bestie Sanaisia only in the bathroom,
She looked like the kind of girl I could hang and rock with.

Many people look at my classes and test scores and
question the people I hang with, I love my weaves, and big
flashy jewelry, but don't get me wrong!

I just know when to turn "it" on and off.

I find it hard in class to be myself,
Coz I'm not that quiet, shy girl you think I am.
Even though I hang out with the geechie and ghetto,
I get my work done hunnnnay!
Coz I'm not bout to look like no...
"Dummmmmey."

An Accomplishment

Shydazja Wright

To me it feels like an accomplishment
Like I worked so hard to finally get to high school
and start my journey.
It is good to finally have some freedom to be finally
treated like a young adult for once.
Grades are important in high school so as long as I
keep my grades up everything should be good.
Thanks to all the teachers that helped me get this far.

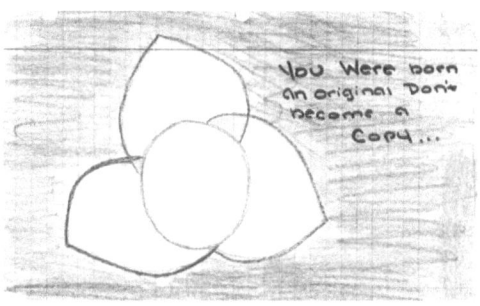

We Are Maturing

Skylar Held

It feels like we are maturing into young men and women
and we are becoming more responsible. Next year will
not be a joke because they do not play around. They
will not feel bad when you mess up and fail. My brother
said it is no joke, so I am not going to mess around next
year and I am not going to worry about anything other
than my grades.

Success

Patrick Myers

School isn't something everyone wants to do. We have to.
We benefit from it in many ways we don't understand.
Even if we are arguing or trying to take a stand,
School will evolve you into a better man

We all go to college to get better knowledge.
Sometimes we're scared to ask questions
When we don't have the feel of protection
But somehow we keep pushing in the right direction.

When you arrive at college, you have to adjust.
Sharing the rest room with 20 other guys will create a mess.
Having no one to support you can make you up set.
You just feel like quitting, I bet.

Sometimes you have to believe in yourself.
Say you can do anything you put your mind to.
Even if your mom has to remind you.
When you ask for a job no one can decline you

You have no help financially,
So you have to cry and plea,
But it's simply paper money.
But in college money is key.

You overcome a lot of obstacles.
You wish you had done some things differently.
Like asking better questions than can I go pee.
Hopefully you graduated and turned out successfully.

Crunch Time

Tremell Bowens

To know that you will go to places with more freedom
and opportunities.

As you go through the hard times you know
what you are shooting for.

Your future depends on what you make of this time.
The decisions you make everyday will reflect
on you in the future.

Many different classes, no more nice teachers
to walk you though.

It's the real crunch time.

Written from an Interviewee's Point of View

Kayla Cannady

College wasn't a priority but a way to attain my dreams
They told you the pros and cons
That it's not always what it seems
Attending an online college
Who said it'd be easier than so
Lots of effort is just as needed.
So is it easy? I'd say "no."

A family to take care of
Feeling pressured and caught,
Working hard night and day,
Trying to keep a positive thought.

I hoped college secured a good job.
One that would provide well
It was still hard to find jobs.
Which ones were good? It was hard to tell.

Then one day I finally realized...
The job I was aiming for
Could separate me and my family,
So I looked for another "open door."

Even though I didn't proceed,
I'm still where I needed to be.
My love for education remains.
But I'm proudly with my family.

Fire Marshall

Mackenzie Cook

Living in Charleston his whole life,
Ted traveled the world.
He went to England in the military,
And met his future wife.

After the military,
He went to Mississippi to learn.
Taking many courses at different schools.
Getting good grades.

During college, what did he do?
Get engaged to the English woman.
They got married and now,
He has more responsibilities.

With his religion teachers voice in his head
He saw the world in a different light.
The bible made more sense.
He understood different cultures better.

With good memories from college,
Like the time he brought his dog to class,
He graduated with honor roll grades.

Ted knew he would be in the fire service.
College helped him reach his dream.
He became a Fire Marshall himself.
Proud of his achievements.

The Sound of the Last Bell...

Briashmel Bell

I've been at JZMS since the middle sixth grade,
And I will have to say,
Although I'm ready for high school,
I kind of want to stay.

The teachers have taught me much
I still have more to learn
I'm also Ms. Lightning
That spot I earned.

I'll also miss the people.
Sheniah, Taniah, and more.
I'm sure that I'll still see them.
When I do we'll turn up some more.

Then there's the sports.
Tennis, Cheer, and Basketball.
Talking at lunch and recess.
Playing in the halls.

Here's a list about Zucker Middle School
Of things that I'll miss.

Oh I forgot one thing...
The sound of the last bell...

"Ring Ring Ring..."

Epilogue

It has been a long road, indeed. A road fraught with pit stops and potholes...stumbling points and finish lines...deadlines missed and understandings forgotten...with a storied past and a love of reading and writing.

That could be the beginning of any volume of student writing from almost any middle school in the country, I suppose. How boring, you must be thinking.

The story of Zuckerbook is anything but boring. It is a tale (not sordid) of many minds over many years coming together at the right place and the right time. It is the story of many students, present and past, who love to write and read (even if many of them don't really know it). It is the story of three previous books created in different times in different places for the same reasons.

It all started with "321." I threw that together at the last minute, wanting to create a gift for the students of my very first 8th grade class, way back when I was a graduate student at Lewis and Clark College. It was an intense experience, to say the least, and a tremendous amount of work for one person to undertake. I remember with fondness how excited many of them were to contribute the piece of their choice...mysteries, essays, poems, whatever. They were ecstatic at the idea of seeing their work in print, and that experience stuck with me. I knew that, if given another chance, I would do this again, and when that happened, I would involve the students in the production of the book.

Then, a year of private teaching and a move across the country later, I teamed up with Ms. Douglas in my second year at Zucker Middle School and, in the fall of 2011, we threw together an after school class with three students who were probably more interested in doing anything but working on a book and gave it a go.

We collected whatever we could find, contributed a few pieces of our own, and went for it. An entire day was spent typing things by various students in various classes and typeset by yours truly on an old Power-book that had survived two runs of graduate school, a novel, and a cross-country voyage. The result was "Dude, It's a Magazine," and, all things considered, it was pretty good.

The following year, which was 2012-2013, we teamed up again and decided that we needed a different format. We wanted more of a book, and less time using my old comb binder. We again ran an after school club dedicated to producing our literary magazine, this time with more enthusiastic students. More teachers involved themselves in contrib-uting student work, and more artwork was included. We sought the help of a graphic design studio and found an excellent match in Bridget Means, Creative Director of September Design Studios. She took our stacks of pages and piles of images and helped us assemble a real identity for our book of student writing, complete with a logo and a slogan and a profes-sional layout. We still had to assemble it by hand – our laser printers were going full bore for three days, and we stapled them together ourselves. The result was "Zuckerbook," and it was truly a remarkable feat. I scat-tered them all over the school and around the community, swelling with pride and excitement. We did it! We created a real book!

There was much rejoicing. We did the whole thing on a shoestring budget (read: Sarah and I paid for it ourselves) and it was great.

The following year, however, was not so good for Zuckerbook. Many students inquired about the club, but no one joined. Ms. Douglas had moved on to loftier climes and a highly coveted teaching position in a highly successful high school in Charlotte, NC. There were few if any resources to create another volume of Zuckerbook, and without a student staff, it felt like an impossible task. I collected writing anyway, but did not produce the second volume of Zuckerbook.

And then this year came along. I still had tons of writing left over

from the year before. I started the club again and received almost no interest. It started to look like Zuckerbook might have been a "one hit wonder."

And then, over the Winter Break, I got to thinking. How could I
assemble an almost hand-picked group of students to assemble the next
Zuckerbook without having to do it after school? How could I get them to
do most of the work themselves? How could I find the cash to produce
a real paperback book? My Cultural Anthropology class was the answer
to all of these questions. It was fun, we had done some really cool and
creative things in that class, but did I really want to teach it again? No, not
really. It was a "Z" period elective class that was a ton of fun, but it was
also the only way I could possibly run Zuckerbook as a class, during the
school day, with enough students to staff a small company dedicated to
our cause.

I took that class and divided it into teams – fund raising, internal
production, external production, and public relations. I lifted a note or two
from my colleague and dear friend, Mr, Aiello, and assigned team leaders
and gave them projects to assign to their teams. I dug out my collection of
student work, assigned more creative writing, had them plunder the blog
(my after school homework site) for more creative work, and had them
chase after teachers for artwork and writing. We started strategizing creat-
ing a paperback book of student writing, looked at costs and budgets,
ways to raise funds, and ways to raise awareness for our project. With
a stumble and a sputter, we got started. I baked cookies, with the much
appreciated assistance of my spouse, and we sold them as cookie grams
for Valentine's Day and St. Patrick's Day. I accepted donations from students a dollar at a time and spiffed them cookies and cans of soda for their
trouble. We started a GoFundMe page that has largely been ignored and
found our way to Facebook. I posted a few choice words here and there
out in the social media universe and received a couple of generous donations. All of this brought us to far more than our initial (laughable) goal of
2,500.00, as well as a long list of "How To Do This Right" and "What Not To
Do" and "What We Should Have Done Differently." It was a learning experience for myself as well as my staff, and we all grew a great deal as a result.

Now, as I work with September Design Studio to typeset and layout the book you now hold in your hands, seeing everything that we could have done differently and all of the things we never got around to doing, I realize that I wouldn't change a thing. This book represents an astounding series of firsts, for myself, for my students, and for our school, and it has been an absolute honor to be a part of it.

And, I know, the real work is about to begin. We have promotional materials to produce. We have to get this book out in shops and for sale online. We have to promote our efforts and distribute copies to those folks who generously donated time and effort to our cause. We have to now fulfill our promise of elevating the profile of our school and our community by "getting this thing out there," as I have said many times to the staff. We have another quarter to finish, as of this writing, and there is a ton of work to do. I can hardly wait to see how all of this turns out. Further, I can hardly wait to see what happens next. Future plans include putting together our own non-profit organization and expanding our publishing base to include collections of student work from other schools in our district, and even to publish works from unsung student authors in our community. Onward and upward, as I used to say, because there is nowhere else to go.

I do hope you are enjoying the fruits of our labors, and have developed a vivid picture of the people involved in The Zuckerbook Project. Without a doubt, it has been a labor of love for everyone involved, a true community project assembled by the great people who hang their hats at Zucker Middle School.

I can hardly wait until next year.

With gratitude, a tip of the hat, and a big ol' smile...

Erik J. Hilden
April 2nd, 2015